Blame
It on the
B₃raiN₂?

Resources for Changing Lives

A series published in cooperation with
THE CHRISTIAN COUNSELING AND EDUCATIONAL FOUNDATION,
Glenside, Pennsylvania

Susan Lutz, Series Editor

Available in the series:

Edward T. Welch, *When People Are Big and God Is Small: Overcoming Peer Pressure, Codependency, and the Fear of Man*

Paul David Tripp, *Age of Opportunity: A Biblical Guide to Parenting Teens*

Edward T. Welch, *Blame It on the Brain? Distinguishing Chemical Imbalances, Brain Disorders, and Disobedience*

James C. Petty, *Step by Step: Divine Guidance for Ordinary Christians*

Paul David Tripp, *War of Words: Getting to the Heart of Your Communication Struggles*

Edward T. Welch, *Addictions—A Banquet in the Grave: Finding Hope in the Power of the Gospel*

Paul David Tripp, *Instruments in the Redeemer's Hands: People in Need of Change Helping People in Need of Change*

David Powlison, *Seeing with New Eyes: Counseling and the Human Condition through the Lens of Scripture*

Blame
It on the
BraiN?

Distinguishing Chemical Imbalances,
Brain Disorders, and Disobedience

EDWARD T. WELCH

P U B L I S H I N G
P.O. BOX 817 • PHILLIPSBURG • NEW JERSEY 08865-0817

Unless otherwise indicated, Scripture quotations are from the HOLY BIBLE, NEW INTERNATIONAL VERSION. Copyright © 1973, 1978, 1984 International Bible Society. Used by permission of Zondervan Bible Publishers. *Italics (or reverse italics) indicate emphasis added.*

Composition by Colophon Typesetting

Printed in the United States of America

Library of Congress Cataloging-in-Publication Data

Welch, Edward T., 1953–
    Blame it on the brain? : distinguishing chemical imbalances, brain disorders, and disobedience / Edward T. Welch.
        p.   cm. — (Resources for changing lives)
    Includes biblographical references (p.).
    ISBN-10: 0-87552-602-0
    ISBN-13: 978-0-87552-602-7
    1. Brain—Diseases—Religious aspects—Christianity.
2. Neuropsychiatry.   I. Title.   II. Series.
    RC386.2.W43   1998
    616.8—dc21   98-7094

To John Bettler,

the head and heart of the

Christian Counseling and Educational Foundation,

Glenside, Pennsylvania

Contents

ACKNOWLEDGMENTS

MANY thanks to my colleagues at the Christian Counseling and Educational Foundation (CCEF), whose names could just as easily have appeared on the cover. John Bettler, David Powlison, and Paul Tripp continually shape my theological thought and academic direction. Not only they, but the entire CCEF staff and board made this possible through their support, prayer, and personal sharpening.

Susan Lutz, my coworker and editor, is the total package: wordsmith, a walking Strunk and White, cultural analyst, theologian, and counselor. Many thanks—again.

My students in "Counseling and Physiology" at Westminster Theological Seminary and Biblical Theological Seminary always have great ideas, case studies, insights, and questions. Thank you.

My wife, Sharon, is the one who keeps my theology practical. It is great to have a companion whose strengths cover my weaknesses and whose love covers my sins.

INTRODUCTION

THE 1990s were officially declared the decade of the brain, and for good reason.

> ➤ President Reagan's Alzheimer's disease brought to national attention a disabling brain disease that creates innumerable practical difficulties and untold pain for hundreds of thousands of families and friends.

> ➤ Researchers offered possible treatments for previously incurable brain diseases.

> ➤ New technologies provided unprecedented views of the brain.

> ➤ Philosophers and theologians rediscovered the mind-body debate.

Given these and hundreds of other events, it is probably more accurate to say that the 1990s were merely the *debut* of influential brain research. Much more is yet to come.

I have been an interested student of the brain ever since I did research in brain diseases and brain electrophysiology in the 1970s. Since then, I have found that a rudimentary understanding of brain functioning can be very useful when it comes to understanding and helping others. For example, a knowledge of brain functioning can help us answer questions about chemical imbalances and the appropriateness of psychiatric medicines. It can help us understand people whose ability to learn and think are different from our own. And it can also help us distinguish between physical and spiritual problems. In the material that follows, I hope to provide some of this helpful information.

Yet, even though I am enthusiastic about understanding brain function, I wonder if the brain has been receiving *too much* credit. Consider, for example, some other "discoveries" of the 1990s that have been more troubling.

➤ Ritalin became *the* prescription for children.

➤ Mood swings that were once seen as a result of a bad day at the office, an afternoon battle with the children, or disappointment in relationships, are now viewed as the result of chemical imbalances in the brain, treated with antidepressant medications or, for those who want more natural assistance, St. John's Wort and other herbs.

➤ We have a growing sense that the brain is the *real* cause of behavior. What started as a suggestion that brain chemistry is the ultimate cause of alcohol abuse has expanded to the point where brain chemistry is considered the ultimate cause for literally every human problem.

Have you ever been surprised at how some people have accused their brain, making it responsible for some of their bad behavior? I once watched a televised press conference given by a prominent politician that made me actually feel sorry for the man's brain. It was declared guilty without any real evidence.

This anti-drug politician had been a Teflon man through his two terms of office. Although he had faced constant legal charges, none of them stuck. Embezzlement, selling political favors, drug use—he was always accused but never found guilty. Now he had been caught in the act of buying and using illegal drugs. It was all on tape. How was he going to get out of it this time?

As he was moving toward the podium, a reporter called out, "Why did you do it? Why did you lie to us all these years?"

His response was immediate. "I didn't do it," he said. "My brain was messed up. It was my brain that did it. My disease did it!" There wasn't a hint of remorse—only indignation that someone would ask such a question.

I had to shake my head as I watched. Surely he could come up with a better answer than that! No real student of the brain would accept such an excuse. I thought, *These reporters will be all over him in a minute with that response.*

But to my surprise, no one was laughing. His answer actually seemed to satisfy everyone present. Maybe they were afraid that they would appear ignorant of some brain research that supported the politician's claims. Maybe they didn't want to attack someone as a villain who might turn out to be a victim. Whatever the case, the politician appeared to have silenced his critics. He was already moving to another topic.

If privately polled, most of those attending the press conference would probably have said that this man was simply trying to avoid blame. But they would have had to give him credit for at least one thing: he knew how to change with the times. A few decades ago, his best bet would have been to blame his upbringing. Now, following some of the cultural trends of the day, he blamed it on his brain. And no one dared challenge him.

This means that the task before us in this book is twofold: to introduce areas where the brain has received too little credit, and to highlight where the brain has received too much credit (or blame).

As human problems seem to get both deeper and more widespread, people are desperate for solutions—and the quicker the better! How wonderful it would be, many think, if the right pill or genetic alteration could solve our problems! And such hope is encouraged by reports suggesting that we are on the verge of revolutionary brain treatments for problems that were once attributed to the soul.

As Christians, we are not so naive, however. We know that we cannot blindly accept everything we hear as God's truth. Information we receive about brain functioning is viewed the same way we view any information, whether it is about finances, parenting, or the causes of our behavior: we view it through the lens of Scripture. And that requires us to be thoughtful, careful, and prayerful as we hear and assess the latest scientific discoveries.

Frankly, many people don't understand why we attempt to do this. They think we are narrow-minded, old-fashioned, paranoid, or—well, you fill in the blanks. Most people are under the impression that researchers go into their laboratories and simply report the facts. Then, those who get those facts report them to us. The reality, however, isn't that simple. Although observations and discoveries come to us garbed in scientific language, they are more than just facts by the time we hear them. The reality is that, like all information we receive, data about the brain is shaped by influences such as our own desires and the unspoken assumptions of our culture.

At best, by the time brain research filters down to us, it is like a message distorted by a long game of "Whisper down the lane." The original brain researcher whispers, "The brain is a remarkable instrument that *participates* in or *contributes* to all behavior." But the last person hears, "My brain made me do it." That's what you and I tend to hear from our neighbors or read in the newspapers. And that was the message the politician used at the press conference to try to keep his job.

Responsible research, of course, does not support the politician's comments, but some research *does* suggest that more and more of our behaviors are caused by brain functioning and dysfunctioning. Probably this evidence started the whispers that, when misinterpreted, led to the politician's excuses.

So here is the problem. Sometimes it is legitimate to blame our misbehaviors on the brain, and sometimes it isn't. How can we know? In the case of the politician, the answer is obvious. But there are other cases, such as those discussed in this book, where the answer is less clear.

To help you think through these issues and questions, Part One of this book will supply the theological resources necessary for dialogue with the brain sciences. Why *theological* resources rather than technological and scientific? Because theology is the lens through which Christians interpret all research, and it is essential that our lens be clear and accurate. Sadly, in relation to the brain sciences, our lenses have been particularly cloudy, and, as a result, they have not controlled our vision. In fact, many people seem to take their biblical lenses off entirely when looking at brain research. Therefore, Part One will clean and polish our theological glasses.

The theological structure presented in Part One is fairly straightforward: we are created by God as a unity of at least two substances—spirit and body. Nothing new here. This is a theological statement that has stood for centuries. What is new, however, is the *application* of this theology to some modern questions.

Outfitted with this theology and its manifold applications, Part Two will put it to work. Part Two will take some modern diagnoses and experiences, all attributed to the brain, and consider them from a biblical perspective. We will not discuss every disease and every experience in detail. Instead, you will learn a *way* of thinking that will allow you to think biblically about specific problems as you encounter them. This, in turn, will enable you to minister biblically, with confidence, wisdom, and compassion.

PART ONE   *Biblical Foundations*

CHAPTER

WHO'S IN CHARGE?

"I think I have a chemical imbalance. What should I do?"

"Should my child be taking Ritalin?"

"Why is my father acting like this? Alzheimer's disease has changed him so much."

"Since his accident, my son has been fired from twenty-five jobs. Is he going to be living with us for the rest of our lives?"

"I'm angry that God made me an alcoholic. Other people don't have to deal with this. Why did he give *me* this disease?"

"It's hard to stop cruising gay bars and getting pornography from the Internet. How *can* I stop when I have a homosexual orientation?"

These are some of the new questions that make helping other people seem more complicated these days. We like to think that the Bible is sufficient for the critical questions of life, but these questions challenge that assumption. After all, what does the Bible have to say about chemical imbalances, Ritalin, and alcoholism as a disease? Maybe every friend, counselor, discipler, and pastor should have their Bible knowledge supplemented by courses in genetics, neurochemistry, and brain injury and disease.

But there is an alternative approach. Consider this: What is needed is not necessarily more sophistication in understanding the brain. Instead, what is needed is a more in-depth and practical examination of Scripture that is relevant to these questions. Then we can use the observations of the brain sciences to illustrate the biblical position.

Our task begins by listening to a discussion that has gone on for centuries. It concerns the soul (also called *mind*), the brain, and how they are related.

The Soul and the Brain

For centuries the brain has been an object of human fascination. "Can this really be the seat of the elusive soul? If so, where exactly *is* the soul?" asked physicians and philosophers. As early as the fifth century B.C., the physician Alkmeon of Kroton proposed a fairly sane theory. He suggested that sensory information such as sight and sound were more earthly and occupied distinct brain areas. Thoughts, on the other hand, were spiritual. They were part of the immortal, immaterial soul and could not be physically located.

Plato declared that the brain was supreme among the organs of the body, but his reasoning was peculiar. He thought that a lower, rounded part of the brain, now called *the medulla,* was where God planted and enclosed the soul. Aristotle was not so sure. He thought that the heart was the place to find the human soul. The brain was merely a type of radiator or "kettle" that either warmed or cooled the blood.

Stratos of Lampsakos found the soul between the eyebrows! Shakespeare, following a Greek philosopher, wrote that the soul was in the pia mater, part of the meningeal skin that covers the brain. In *Troilus and Cressida* (act 2, scene 1) he criticizes Ajax of Thersites: "His pia mater is not worth the ninth part of a sparrow." Most popular was the idea that the soul resided in the fluid-filled ventricles of the brain. The ventricles, some clerics thought, were the one place in the brain that seemed to have enough room to house a soul.

Everybody had a theory about the relationship between the brain and the soul, and most of them were horribly amiss. In fact, it has been suggested that, at least in the brain sciences, "the greatness of a man is solely to be measured by the length of time his ideas impede progress."[1]

Some could argue that such a definition of greatness is still relevant to the brain or neurosciences, but no one can deny the dramatic developments over the past two centuries. This progress can be attributed, in part, to technological advances. Electron microscopes, CT scans, and new imaging devices have created unparalleled windows to the brain. Just a few decades ago we had our first glimpse of the way nerve cells communicated with each other. Now brain research is unraveling the mysteries of the genetic underpinnings of those cells and discovering the scores of chemicals that are the brain's communication network. Armed with this technological sophistication, brain researchers have been able to let their scientific curiosity run wild. The result has been a foundation of pure research that, in the next twenty years, will most likely lead to life-saving advances in diseases such as Parkinson's and Alzheimer's. For brain researchers these are, indeed, "heady" times.

As onlookers who might not know the difference between positron emission tomography and evoked potentials, the extent of our interest in the brain sciences might be to sit on the sidelines and applaud. We don't understand what the brain scientists are doing, but it sounds good, and the occasional comments about the possible applications of the research are particularly encouraging. So we say, "Keep up the good work; may the National Institute of Health grant you more and more money."

This, however, is not saying enough.

---

1   G. W. Bruyn, "The Seat of the Soul," in *Historical Aspects of the Neurosciences*, ed. F. Clifford Rose and W. F. Bynum (New York: Raven Press, 1982), 56.

What Does God's Word Say?

As sophisticated and impressive as the brain sciences are, the premise of this book is that they sit under something even more spectacular. They are under the Bible, and their results should be evaluated through the interpretive grid of biblical categories. This may sound audacious at first. After all, what can the Bible offer the brain sciences, especially considering the patently wrong ideas on the brain and the soul that were prevalent in biblical times? Wouldn't it make more sense to say that the Bible is authoritative on the spiritual realm, and the brain sciences are authoritative on the brain?

It may sound plausible, but such a compromise solution actually demeans the God of Scripture and exalts human insight. It would be like saying, "There are some areas of investigation where I will not first ask, 'What does God say?' " The truth is that all knowledge begins, as Proverbs indicates, with "the fear of the LORD." All knowledge begins by first asking, "What does God say? How does God want us to see this?" This is how we study sex, money and economics, politics, and anything else worthy of careful thought. Everything in life *should* come under the authority of Scripture (Figure 1.1).[2]

The problem in establishing biblical oversight of the brain sciences is that, at first glance, there seem to be very few biblical principles available to guide us. Here are three:

1. God created all things. Therefore, God created the brain.
2. God has called us to be students of creation. Therefore, creation, including the brain, can be studied and partially understood.

---

2 We can, of course, be wrong in our interpretation of Scripture. Scripture is infallible; we, its interpreters, are not. As such, when there is disagreement between Scripture and scientific observations, the problem may lie in the reliability of the scientific observation, our interpretation of Scripture, or both.

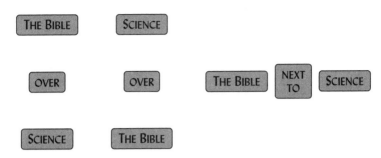

Figure 1.1. Three possible relationships between the Bible and science

3. Students of God's world should be people of integrity or truth-tellers. Therefore, scientists should be careful in their investigations and truthful in their reporting of results. They should not fabricate or skew results to suit their private agendas.

These are good and true principles, but they do not help us bring the wisdom of the Bible into the more technical discussions of the day. The result is that, although in theory we place the Bible over the brain sciences, in practice we do not use God's Word to control the interpretation of neuroscientific data. The Bible winds up looking like a head of state that has no real power—a puppet king at best.

Unfortunately, the Bible has been losing its functional authority in the biological sciences for quite some time. One turning point was the cholera epidemics of the 1800s. During the first two epidemics in 1832 and 1849, the church was considered the epidemic's authoritative interpreter and advisor. Sadly, from this prestigious position, the church came forth with simplistic and incomplete explanations. It usually explained the cholera outbreaks as evidence of divine retribution against sin. This was especially convenient because it was usually the lower classes that were affected, not the financially stable middle and upper class folk who were the typical church members.

While it is true that disease *can* be a result of divine discipline and *can*

23

indicate a need for soul-searching and repentance, it is also true that disease can be unrelated to personal sin. In fact, to say that sickness is *always* a result of personal sin is actually an old heresy that goes back to Job and his counselors. So why didn't the church in the 1800s teach that sin and sickness are not necessarily related? Why didn't it encourage precise observation of the created (though fallen) world in order to more fully understand the epidemics? Perhaps the church's theological lenses were unrefined and unable to interpret those problems meaningfully.

This inaccurate use of Scripture eventually took its toll. By the time of the 1866 cholera epidemic, no one looked to the church for helpful answers. Instead, the focus changed to public health initiatives, and the realm of Scripture's legitimate rule was thereby narrowed. Instead of Scripture over science, science ruled its own kingdom, and Scripture was given a small piece of less-than-prime property.

> God was still in heaven, as most Americans would be quick to affirm. Yet the fact of his existence had ceased to be a central and meaningful reality in their lives. The warnings of the perceptive divines in 1832 were proving justified; material preoccupations and empirical habits of thought had not so much defeated as displaced the spiritual concerns of earlier generations. Americans seemed to be well on the way toward becoming a land of "practical atheists."[3]

Today in the brain sciences the situation is similar. The Bible has not been defeated, but it has become irrelevant. Many researchers find no more use for the idea of an immaterial soul. All our behaviors are allegedly explained by brain chemistry and physics.

3 C. E. Rosenberg, *The Cholera Years* (Chicago: University of Chicago Press, 1962), 213.

Are you familiar with the research on alcoholism? The research itself is fascinating, but it can arrive at our door wrapped in a theory that says there is no soul. Drinking to intoxication is now called a disease that comes from the body, not the soul. If you were to suggest that sin causes drunkenness, you would be greeted in the same way that moderns might greet Stratos of Lampsakos and his eyebrow theory. You would be a curious but irrelevant voice from the past.

Consider some other practical problems. Let's say that a pastor is counseling a female parishioner who is very depressed. For years they struggle together, confident that there are biblical answers to her depression. Then a neighbor of the depressed person happens to mention her own experience with antidepressant medication. The depressed woman goes to her neighbor's psychiatrist, starts taking medication, and her depression lifts. There is no question that this woman will consider the brain sciences to be more insightful and authoritative regarding her problem than the Bible. She had tried both, and medication was more effective.

What about the opening case study in the book *Listening to Prozac*[4]? It describes a man whose interest in pornography ended soon after taking that drug. Do you think this man will ever call pornographic indulgence sin? Clearly not. It was not a spiritual change that removed his desire; it was a medication that manipulated brain chemicals. Therefore, he will argue, if the soul exists, it can be changed through prescription drugs, not preaching the Gospel.

The list can go on. You already know about the debates over the biological basis for homosexuality. Do you realize that anger, disobedience to parents, worry, drug abuse, stealing, and adultery are also being touted as brain problems rather than sin problems? The brain research itself rarely draws these conclusions. But once the research

4 Peter D. Kramer, *Listening to Prozac* (New York: Viking, 1993), ix–xi.

gets whispered down the lane to the six o'clock news and into the popular psyche, it is often surrounded by these interpretations.

As Christians today, we want to avoid the ecclesiastical mistakes of the 1800s. This time, we want to listen to what people are saying about the brain, develop clear and powerful biblical categories, and bless both the sciences and the church in the process.

CHAPTER 2

MIND-BODY:
QUESTIONS AND ANSWERS

Man considering himself is the great prodigy of nature. For he cannot conceive what his body is, even less what his spirit is, and least of all how body can be united with spirit. That is the peak of his difficulty and yet it is his very being. —*Blaise Pascal*

IT is tempting to race immediately to a very practical question: Are there times when, because of my brain, I am not responsible for my behavior? This, indeed, is a critical question. It is a place where the Bible can clarify and sharpen the brain sciences. But in this case, theory should precede practice, because by the time we get to the very practical questions, we have traveled through worlds of assumptions. These underlying assumptions are where we must begin.

Consider this assumption-laden quote from brain researcher Donald O. Hebb: "The idea of an immaterial mind controlling the body has no place in science." He does not speak for everyone in the neurosciences, but he does introduce an essential discussion.[1] What *is* this

---

1 Hebb's statement does not necessarily mean that the immaterial realm does not

thing called *mind* or *soul?* Does it even exist? If so, does mind emerge out of matter (that is, the brain), or is mind different from matter? Such questions may seem a long way from where we live, but they have implications that travel from the laboratory to the court system to the local church. They influence your views on personal responsibility, mental illness, the extent to which the brain determines behavior, and even the afterlife.

This mind-body discussion is especially active today, but it is handicapped from the start. Although a definition of *matter* is clear—it is stuff that takes up physical space—the meaning of the word *mind* is more elusive. As William James said, mind is something the meaning of which "we know as long as no one asks us to define it."

Secular Perspectives on the Mind and Its Relationship to the Body

Philosophers and brain scientists *have* reached a general consensus on a rough definition. They suggest that *mind* has something to do with *consciousness, self-awareness,* or my experience of *me.* It is the recognition that I am an actor rather than something that is simply acted upon by irresistible instincts. It is the sense that I make decisions and have a purpose for what I do. This view of mind assumes the abilities to remember and count, but it is more than those. It is the awareness that *I* remembered my wife's birthday or *I* added these numbers. The mind reflects on itself.

A question on which there is less agreement is this: What is the connection between mind (self-awareness) and matter (chemical activity in the brain)? Are they separate or of the same substance?

---

exist. It means that this realm is not the focus of most science. The focus of science is matter. Science cannot adjudicate spiritual issues. From this perspective, I agree with him. However, this statement is extended to mean that there should be a separation of science and Scripture, with which I would disagree.

Nearly every philosopher and brain scientist has his own theory of the relationship between mind and body. As a whole, these theories loosely cluster into two larger groups. One group is dualistic, suggesting that mind and matter are two different substances. Another group, usually the brain scientists and physicists, are monistic, suggesting that mind emerges out of matter.

Of the dualistic alternatives, perhaps best known to theologians is the so-called animistic hypothesis, the "ghost in the machine." It is the theory in which you would most likely hear about the soul. It assumes that mind is an immaterial force that guides matter. If you take away mind, it says, then matter becomes lifeless.

A second form of dualism is called *interactionism*. It states that the body can influence the mind, and the mind can influence the body. In other words, thoughts and actions can cause brain activity, and brain activity can cause certain behaviors. This view seems to appreciate the unity between the mind and body while it avoids the deterministic tendencies of the monists. It also happens to be similar to the biblical model proposed in the next chapter.

Although there is a grassroots interest in interactionism, monism is winning the day. Since dualistic theories assume an immaterial mind, they are often criticized by the more tough-minded monists. "No spooks" is a basic monistic assumption. "Why," some ask, "do we assume something that is beyond measurement? Doesn't dualism introduce seemingly superfluous spiritual forces into biology?" Monists cite an axiom sometimes called Ockham's Razor. It says this: Given two or more equally likely explanations for an event, take the one that is simplest. Monists suggest that their theory is the most elegant in its simplicity.

Yet monism is not that simple. Like dualism, there are different perspectives within it. The best known assumes that mind is something that matter *does*. Mind *emerges* out of the brain. "The brain secretes thoughts the way the liver secretes bile," or "Behind every crooked thought is a crooked molecule." It is as if the brain casts a shadow that we call consciousness or mind.

This perspective squares with much of the research, but it too leaves us with its own set of questions. For example, what is the purpose of consciousness or self-awareness? What use does it have? What good does it do? In short, why would the brain bother to secrete it? Since monism usually is accompanied by evolutionary assumptions, monists should have an answer to these questions. At this point, however, their predominant response is that consciousness is just a random event that emerged out of the information-processing machines that were the early humans. In other words, mind is a mystery whether you are a dualist or a monist.

A second monistic approach that embraces aspects of dualism suggests that there is one substance that possesses both mental and physical attributes. Electromagnetic fields are cited as a comparable phenomenon. At one time electric and magnetic forces were thought to be distinct entities. Now they are considered to be interrelated manifestations of a single electromagnetic field. Another illustration is how light, being one substance, can function as both particles and waves.

These monistic analogies are interesting but are still too technical to help most of us understand the mind-brain relationship. Analogies attempt to describe something complicated (the mind-body relationship) in terms of something simpler (the physics of light and electromagnetism). But in this case, the analogies are as complex as the phenomenon they attempt to clarify, and thus less helpful for most of us.

In the midst of this debate, what is a Christian supposed to think? Theologians have usually been in favor of some version of dualism, but there have been increasing numbers of Bible scholars who have joined the monistic camp. This is because the evidence in support of monism is strong. Almost everything that was once considered to be the purview of the immaterial spirit or soul is now clearly seen to be under the control of the brain. For example, speech, personality, emotions, intellectual ability, and even will are actually under the authority of the brain. How do we know? Look at people who have suffered severe brain injury. They might be unable to speak, their personalities might be very different, their emotions fluctuate without provocation, and they are intellectually less competent. All these abilities are directly dependent on and emerge out of brain functioning.

Given these facts, is there anything left for the soul? It seems not. No wonder that when *Newsweek* asked the question, "Is the mind an illusion?" the answer was "Yes, say the philosopher-scientists. The brain is a machine. We have no selves, no souls."[2]

A Biblical Perspective on the Mind and Its Relationship to the Body

To enter this debate, there are three questions that we must first consider.

1. Is there really a distinct spiritual substance? Do we, in fact, have an immaterial soul, or is the soul an artifact of Greek thought?
2. If there is such a thing as a spirit or soul, then how would we define it? What does it do?
3. If there is spiritual substance, how does it relate to or interact with the physical substance of the person?

---

2 "Is the Mind an Illusion?" *Newsweek,* 20 April 1992, 70–71. But the editors were not fully persuaded that the monists won. To show that the debate was far from over, they ended with another question. "How do they [the philosopher-scientists] know? Well, it's just a matter of faith."

Chapter Two

Are We More Than a Physical Body?

These questions eventually move us into mysteries, yet there are also some clear and unequivocal biblical answers. The most obvious of these answers is that Scripture teaches that the created universe consists of material *and* immaterial substance. Regardless of how many times we go back and recheck our interpretation, the Bible confidently affirms the existence of immaterial substance as well. To become a thoroughgoing materialist would be to deny the existence of God, because God himself is spirit.

> *You saw no form of any kind the day the LORD spoke to you at Horeb out of the fire. Therefore watch yourselves very carefully, so that you do not become corrupt and make for yourselves an idol, an image of any shape, whether formed like a man or a woman, or like any animal on earth or any bird that flies in the air, or like any creature that moves along the ground or any fish in the water below. (Deut. 4:15–18)*

Although a belief in both God and an immaterial, spiritual world is unfashionable among some people, it is safe to say that the majority of the world's population are convinced of the presence of an immaterial world. In fact, given the number of Buddhists and Hindus in the world, we must admit that the majority of people would say that *only* mind exists and *matter* is an illusion! This, of course, does not prove the presence of the spiritual realm. Such issues are not decided by popular vote. But it does suggest that our assumption of an immaterial soul should not be quickly dismissed.

This is the Bible's most relevant teaching on the brain sciences: the created world consists of the spiritual and physical, mind and matter. Human beings in particular are a unity consisting of these two parts.

I belong, body and soul, in life and in death, to my faithful Savior Jesus Christ. (Heidelberg Catechism, Q. 1)

The bodies of men, after death, return to the dust, and see corruption; but their souls, which neither sleep nor die, having immortal substance, immediately return to God. (Westminster Confession 32.1)

We are "composite beings—a natural organism tenanted by, or in a state of symbiosis with, a supernatural spirit."[3] We are spiritual beings clothed in an earthly tent (2 Cor. 5:1). This duality or duplex is introduced almost immediately in the Bible. God made man out of two substances: dust and spirit (Gen. 2:7). This distinction is then assumed and elaborated upon throughout the Old and New Testaments.

If it were his [God's] intention
and he withdrew his spirit and breath,
all mankind would perish together
and man would return to the dust. (Job 34:14–15)

... the dust returns to the ground it came from,
and the spirit returns to God who gave it. (Eccl. 12:7)

Do not be afraid of those who kill the body but cannot kill the soul. Rather, be afraid of the one who can destroy both soul and body in hell. (Matt. 10:28)

For physical training is of some value, but godliness [spiritual training] has value for all things, holding promise for both the present life and the life to come. (1 Tim. 4:8)

3 C. S. Lewis, *Miracles* (New York: Macmillan, 1960), 126.

Admittedly, it seems strange to consider ourselves as a duplex of tangible bodies and intangible spirits. In fact, it *should* seem strange to compartmentalize ourselves that way. After all, we are one person.[4]

> The spirit was once not a garrison, maintaining its post with difficulty in a hostile Nature [body], but was fully "at home" with its organism, like a king in his own country or a rider on his own horse—or better still, as the human part of a Centaur was "at home" with the equine part.[5]

Body and spirit were once seamlessly joined together. But aren't there times when the seam becomes a little more obvious? For example, we talk about an arm or a foot as "my arm" and "my foot," as if they were our possessions. Somehow, our physical being doesn't fully define me. Instead, it *belongs* to me.

This elusive "me" has also been noticed in the medical realm. While the body obviously can be easily seen, the "I" is physically elusive. That is, you can't find it in the brain. For example, there have been brain surgeries where surgeons have had opportunities to electrically stimulate the brains of alert patients. This electrical stimulation can elicit body movements, memories, emotions, and other cognitive activities, yet electrically stimulated activity is always distinguished from "me." Patients have said, after a surgeon's electrode revives forgotten memories or provokes sudden movements, "I didn't do that. You did. I didn't make that sound. You pulled it out of me."[6] The "I" seems to escape all attempts to be physically located.

4 For a fuller theological discussion of the mind-body debate in theological circles, see John Cooper, *Body, Soul, and Life Everlasting* (Grand Rapids: Eerdmans, 1989).

5 C. S. Lewis, *The Weight of Glory and Other Addresses* (Grand Rapids: Eerdmans, 1949), 126.

6 W. Penfield, *The Mystery of the Mind* (Princeton, N.J.: Princeton University Press, 1975).

Also notice how the Christian description of death assumes that we are two substances. Death is when body and spirit are torn from each other. It is when the unseen boundary between body and spirit becomes most apparent: the body wastes away in death, but the spirit survives. If there were no death or physical weakness, the distinctions between body and spirit would be sufficiently blurred as to make them appear functionally indivisible. Since the fall, however, even though these substances belong together, they are capable of separation. Therefore, although Scripture emphasizes that the true person is the whole person—a unity of spirit and body—in our fallen world we must reckon with our twofold nature and its various implications.

What Is the Spirit?

The questions now become a little more difficult. Having briefly reviewed the assumption that we are a unity of two substances, and having determined that the church is on solid ground with this doctrine, the next question is to define, describe, and name our immaterial substance.

A popular name for the immaterial stuff of the person is the spirit, but that is certainly not the only biblical name. Since the Bible has so much to say about our spiritual nature, it provides a rich and diverse vocabulary for it.

In the Bible, "spirit" (*pneuma*) shares its field of meaning with a number of words. Included are terms such as "heart" (*kardia*), "mind" (*dianoia, phrenes,* and *nous*), "soul" (Greek: *psuche.* Hebrew: *nephesh*), "conscience" (*suneidesis*), "inner self" (1 Peter 3:4), and "inner man" (2 Cor. 4:16). Even though these words have different emphases, they can be used almost interchangeably—and I will use them that way.

The basic idea behind all these terms is that every human being lives as a morally responsible creature before the face of God. We have a pervasive Godward orientation. Everything we do is related to the living God.

> The heart in the Scripture is variously used; sometimes for the mind and understanding, sometimes for the will, sometimes for the affections, sometimes for the conscience, sometimes for the whole soul. Generally, it denotes the whole soul of man and all the faculties of it, not absolutely, but as they are all one principle of moral operations, as they concur in our doing good or evil. . . . the seat and subject of the law of sin is the heart of man.[7]

If you obey God's Word, you are witnessing the heart (spirit, mind) in action. If you live as if God is distant and uninvolved in your daily affairs, you are witnessing the heart in action. If you are an avowed atheist, you are witnessing the heart in action. The heart can be seen in the way you do the dishes, the way you live when no one is watching, and the way you love your neighbor. Our hearts are at the center of an ongoing moral drama: Will we live for God or against God? Will we love and worship him or will we love our own desires? It is especially revealed in our answer to the question Jesus posed to Peter, "Do you love me?"

This biblical perspective on the mind (*dianoia*) makes it quite different from its secular namesake. The biblical perspective includes that idea of mind-as-self-aware and mind-as-purposeful, but it is much more. With our minds *we are responsible before God and we respond to him, either for or against.* Our minds are the initiators of all moral action.

---

7 J. Owen, *Temptation and Sin* (Evansville, Ind.: Sovereign Grace Book Club, 1958), 170.

Do not conform any longer to the pattern of this world, but be transformed by the renewing of your mind. Then you will be able to test and approve what God's will is.... (Rom. 12:2)

I pray also that the eyes of your heart [dianoia] may be enlightened in order that you may know the hope to which he has called you.... (Eph. 1:18)

They are darkened in their understanding [dianoia] and separated from the life of God because of the ignorance that is in them due to the hardening of their hearts. (Eph. 4:18)

Once you were alienated from God and were enemies in your minds because of your evil behavior. (Col. 1:21)

This means that there are at least three different definitions of the word *mind*. Philosophically, it refers to self-consciousness and purposeful behavior. Popularly, it refers to intellectual activities, as in, "She has a good mind." Biblically, it is the initiator of all moral action.

In order to avoid confusing the biblical *mind* with the secular, I will often use the terms *spirit* (*spiritual*), *heart*, and *inner person* or *inner self*. The word *heart* is an especially useful synonym. Even in its popular use it is associated with the most central, guiding aspect of the person. When people ask, "What do you really believe in your heart?" they are interested in understanding your deepest, most cherished beliefs. From a biblical perspective, the heart is called "the wellspring of life" that morally guides the entire person (Prov. 4:23).

Using the word *heart* also avoids the association of *mind* with raw intellectual abilities. From a biblical perspective, intellectual abilities actually fit more in the category of the brain than the heart. Memory, logic, and academic abilities are not, in themselves, moral functions.

The heart is the moral helmsman that empowers, initiates, and directs the course of the intellect, but it is not identical to the intellect. This is why the heart or biblical mind is never called "stupid" or "brilliant." The heart can be taught (e.g., 2 Tim. 3:16), but the teaching it needs is the Gospel of Christ, and the faculty by which it learns is faith. Responsiveness then produces character, not intelligence. As the heart abides in Christ by faith, it can be honest and good (Luke 8:15), perfect (Ps. 101:2), single (Jer. 32:39), wise (Job 9:4), and meek (Matt. 11:29–30). Left to itself, it is full of unbelief and is called "calloused" (Acts 28:27), "stubborn" (Mark 3:5), "of stone" (Ezek. 11:19), "deceit[ful]," and "evil" (Prov. 12:20). But its deepest need is not education. Rather, the heart or mind must be made new by redemptive grace through a response of faith (Jer. 24:7; Ps. 51:10).

The good news about this distinction between heart and intellect is that the heart can be renewed and thereby reflect the light of Christ even when the brain is weak or wasting away (2 Cor. 4:16). Therefore, those whose brains are still immature, such as children, can know Christ and follow him in obedience. Those with brain diseases can respond to God. Those who are mentally retarded can be wiser than the scholar. Spirit-given faith, not IQ, is the power behind true knowledge and understanding, and faith is an expression of the heart.

Of course, intellectual understanding is part of faith, but even people with severely damaged intellects have an inherent moral sensitivity. They can know God, they can respond to God, and they have a knowledge of right and wrong. This truth contains a profound blessing. It means that we can reflect the light of Christ even when our brains and other body organs are unhealthy or diseased.

This biblical understanding of the mind or heart creates a strange twist in a dialogue with monists. It means that the Bible actually supports many of the monists' interpretations. The abilities that monists suggest emerge out of brain activity are, in fact, caused by the brain:

this would include reason, conceptual abilities, and many other processes we consider distinctively human.

We would add, however, that monists have not looked at everything. They have not looked at the fact that we can respond to God and are responsible before him. They have not looked at our innate knowledge of God and our knowledge of right and wrong. They have not looked at moral behavior: behavior that would be called sinful because it either violates God's laws or does not measure up to the requirements of God's law; or behavior that would be called godly, good, righteous, or fruit of the Spirit. All these are the domain of the human heart.

What Is the Body?

We now move to the question, How do the immaterial spirit/heart and the material body relate to each other? But before we do, let's briefly consider the body.

The body is the physical aspect of the person, the stuff you can touch, the "outer man"—brain, muscle, organs, bones, and nerve cells. Unfortunately, this has not always earned the body much respect. The body was a house of detention for the soul, according to the Greek Philolaus. Epictetus was ashamed to have a body and called himself a "poor soul shackled to a corpse." "Disdain the flesh," said Marcus Aurelius, "blood and bones and network, a twisted skein of nerves, veins, arteries."[8]

The Bible disagrees. No second class citizen, the body is a "temple of the Holy Spirit" (1 Cor. 6:19) and is indispensable to the activity of the heart. Without it we would have no access to the physical world and we simply would not be persons. Accordingly, Paul could not imagine a person without a corporeal nature (1 Cor. 15). The whole person con-

8 W. Barclay, *Flesh and Spirit* (London: SCM, 1962), 10–11.

sists of body and heart together. Both are essential and neither can function in the material realm in isolation of the other.

One reason why some people think that the body is evil in Scripture involves the use of the word "flesh" (*sarx*).[9] "Flesh" may be used as a synonym for "body" (*soma*). In these cases the flesh might be weak but it is never the human source of evil (see e.g., John 6:53; Rom. 2:28; Gal. 4:13; Eph. 5:31). At other times, especially in the Pauline letters, the word translated "flesh" refers *not* to the body but to the acts of the sinful nature and is contrasted with the Spirit (Rom. 8:4; Gal. 5:17). This failure to distinguish between these two meanings of "flesh" is one reason some people suggest that the body is evil.

The unique contribution of the body to the whole person is that it is the *mediator* of moral action rather than the *initiator*. In a sense, it is equipment for the heart. It does what the heart tells it to do; it is the heart's *vehicle* for concrete ministry and service in the material world. In this capacity, it is not the source of sin and is never called sinful.[10] Instead, the body can be

➤ strong and healthy;

➤ physically weak (Greek: *asthenia*), ill, fragile ("jars of clay"), decaying, and limited;

➤ physically dependent in that it has natural desires that want to be satisfied.

9 The physical body is represented in the Bible by various Hebrew and Greek words. In the Septuagint and Greek New Testament it is usually a translation of the Greek words *soma* (body), *sarx* (flesh), and *melos* (members). (Old Testament Hebrew words for body include *basar, gab, gev, geviyyah, guphah, geshem, nebelah*). Most often, "body" is a translation of *soma* (cf., psycho*somatic*) in which case it consistently refers to the physical body. Other words for the body do not have the same technical consistency as *soma*.

10 Romans 7:14–25 might be raised as evidence against this position, but John

Consider these three characteristics for a moment. It is self-evident that the body can be strong and healthy or weak and ill. In these conditions the body can certainly influence the heart. Health or illness both demand a response from the heart; the heart cannot be indifferent to either. When the body is healthy, the inner person or heart can praise God for his gift of health, or the inner person can respond in pride and forget God's provision. When the body is weak or physically ill, the inner person can either declare that it is strong in the Lord (2 Cor. 12:10), or it can become embittered against God.

Another aspect of bodily weakness is that the body imposes *limitations* on the desires of the heart. For example, I may want to memorize the entire Bible, but my body imposes memory limitations. I may want to stay up all night and pray, but my body wants sleep. I may want to visit the sick, but I may be an invalid myself. Such weakness is not sinful. It is the result of living as a creature in a fallen body.

Another use of *weak* has been less clearly developed, but it has important implications for areas such as addictions: the body is *dependent* or weak in that it has needs and natural desires, such as those for food and rest. If these desires are not met, the body will die. The problem is that these natural physical desires can be caught up in a battle between the inner person and sin. Sin preys upon these natural weaknesses, hoping that the inner person will indulge them rather than exert godly self-control. If the inner person yields to sin, then bodily passions will rule the entire person, and Satan has accomplished a kind of anthropological reversal: the body will control the heart rather

---

Murray, in his commentary on Romans, provides this interpretation: "...we are not to suppose that 'the law of sin' springs from or has its seat in the physical. It would merely indicate...that the apostle brings to the forefront the concrete and overt ways in which the law of sin expresses itself and that our physical members cannot be divorced from the operation of the law of sin."

than the heart control the body. When this relationship is reversed, chaos reigns.

> If your body makes all the decisions and gives all the orders, and if you obey, the physical can effectively destroy every other dimension of your personality. Your emotional life will be blunted and your spiritual life will be stifled and ultimately will become anemic.[11]

This does not mean that the body is evil. It means that sin tries to take advantage of any weakness. For example, the normal and appropriate bodily desire for food, when dominated by sin, can become a ruling desire that takes the form of anorexia, bulimia, or gluttony. Also, the natural bodily desire for sleep and rest, when taken off guard by sin, can move toward laziness. Likewise, drug abuse and sexual sin, both of which have bodily components, are examples of the body's being dominated by sin.

First Corinthians 6:12–20 illustrates the importance of not giving way to bodily desires. In this passage, the apostle Paul mentions two popular mottoes of the day. The first, "Everything is permissible for me," was probably an expression of the freedom that Christians had from the Jewish ceremonial laws. But Paul was concerned about the interpretation of this expression. Permission, when viewed apart from faith, could become license not only to eat everything, but also to participate in sexual sin. "After all," the sinful logic went, "God is saying that we do not have to deny the body any longer."

To preempt this thinking, Paul adds, "but not everything is beneficial," and "I will not be mastered by anything." Paul is warning that the unrighteous heart is prone to lust, and when lust encounters the

11 M. Quoist, *The Christian Response* (Dublin: Gill & Macmillan, 1965), 4.

weaknesses of the body, it can exalt bodily passions so that they master or rule the entire person.

In 1 Corinthians 9:24–27, Paul provides an example of how to deal with the body.

> Do you not know that in a race all the runners run, but only one gets the prize? Run in such a way as to get the prize. Everyone who competes in the games goes into strict training. They do it to get a crown that will not last; but we do it to get a crown that will last forever. Therefore I do not run like a man running aimlessly; I do not fight like a man beating the air. No, I beat my body and make it my slave so that after I have preached to others, I myself will not be disqualified for the prize.

"Sin shall not be your master, because you are not under law, but under grace" (Rom. 6:14). Sin is a usurper with no rightful claim. So, with assurance of "no condemnation" and the knowledge of God's power in us, we are called by God's Word to self-control and discipline through faith (1 Thess. 4:4). As Paul indicates, "I beat my body and make it my slave." This is not asceticism or physical self-denial; rather, it is Paul's response to Satan's tendency to prey on the natural weaknesses and desires of the body.

Applying the Definitions of the Heart and the Body

The biblical categories of heart and body can be put to work in a number of ways. For example, these categories allow us to distinguish between sin and sickness.

> ➤ Any behavior that does not conform to biblical commands or any behavior that transgresses biblical prohibitions proceeds from the heart and is sin.

➤ Any behavior that is more accurately called a weakness proceeds from the body and is sickness or suffering. Sickness or suffering can also be caused by specific sin, but we must be very careful to have ample justification before we make such a link.

These two definitions have also helped us to correctly classify thinking, reasoning, memory, and other cognitive or intellectual processes. These abilities refuse to be forced into the biblical category of *heart* because the Bible does not command people to have infallible memories or perfect scores on math tests. If it were morally wrong to answer "$5 \times 5 = 30$," then intellect would be a function of the heart or mind. The student should repent from the error. But unless mistakes are caused by carelessness, they are not immoral. Instead, they reflect our creaturely limitations—limitations that fit neatly into the category *body.* Cognitive functions can be weakened and "waste away," as in diseases such as Alzheimer's. Affected persons can no longer reason effectively, remember, or plan. As their body (i.e., brain) is affected, their cognitive functions are similarly weakened.

What about our emotions? Are they related more to the heart or the body? A brief response is that emotions are typically a response of the entire person, heart *and* body. But they can proceed from *either* the heart or the body. Depression, for example, when traceable to personal sin or guilt, is caused by the heart. Yet in future chapters we will see that depression can also be caused by bodily weakness.

What about other symptoms, such as hallucinations? Do they reveal a spiritual problem, a physical problem, or both? To answer this question, simply apply the test: Does the Bible *prohibit* hallucinations? The answer is clearly no. Therefore, we don't rebuke people for having hallucinations, we have compassion for them. Although some people may respond sinfully to their hallucinations, or their hallucinations may have been caused by a sinful choice to take certain drugs, hallucinations themselves are not sinful. They are a result of bodily weakness.

Here is a list of other symptoms that can initially be categorized as physical or spiritual.

BODY	HEART (MIND)
Broken bones	*Sin*: sexual immorality, lust, evil
Atherosclerosis	desires, filthy language, malice,
Mental retardation	greed, anger, rage, murder,
Feelings of depression	strife, arrogance, boasting, dis-
Feelings of panic	obedience to parents, unbelief,
Remembering and forgetting	jealousy, gossip, drunkenness,
Hallucinations	lying, idolatry, pride.
Ability to read	
Ability to calculate	*Righteousness (fruits of the*
Problems with attention and	*Spirit)*: patience, love, joy, peace,
concentration	gentleness, kindness, faithful-
Mental confusion	ness, forgiveness, wholesome
Fatigue	speech.

How Do the Heart and Body Relate to Each Other?

With biblically based definitions of the heart and body in hand, we are ready to discuss the most complex question that faces those who think about the brain. That is, how do these different substances relate? How do the two become one?

There are mysteries inherent in any discussion of the unity of heart and body. If you crave precision and completeness, you will be disappointed. As MacDonald Critchley, the famous British neurologist, said, "We must admit that the divine banquet of the brain was, and still is, a feast with dishes that remain elusive in their blending, and with sauces whose ingredients are even now a secret."[12] Mind-brain unity can only be discussed with analogies and metaphors.

The most common metaphor to describe the unity of heart and body is the computer: the body is the hardware, the heart is the software, and both are necessary for operation. This metaphor has aspects of truth in that it illustrates the initiating action of the heart, but it is somewhat dissatisfying. It seems too mechanical. It simply does not capture the mystery and beauty of the unity of heart and body.

Even more powerful, perhaps, are analogies already in Scripture. One that comes immediately to mind is the relationship between husband and wife. Although this analogy, like all analogies, breaks down significantly at certain points, it at least suggests that there is precedent for saying that we can simultaneously be both two and one. It also points to an even greater mystery.

> "For this reason a man will leave his father and mother and be united to his wife, and the two will become one flesh." This is a profound mystery—but I am talking about Christ and the church. (Eph. 5:31–32)

The relationship between Christ and the church is a delightful and intriguing picture of the unity between two distinct substances. Christ is obviously different from and separate from his church, but we are members of Christ's body (1 Cor. 12) and, by faith, are one with him (Rom. 6). We are in him and he is in us. What is his is ours. Anticipated by the created world, this relationship is beautifully illustrated by the vine and the branches (John 15). Jesus is the grapevine, we are the branches or shoots that are inseparable and indistinguishable from the vine.

---

12 M. Critchley, *The Divine Banquet of the Brain* (Philadelphia: Lippincott-Raven, 1979), 267.

Another analogy is the Trinity. The difference here is that there is a unity and distinction among *three* personal beings. God is simultaneously three and one. The three persons, of equal moral and divine excellence, have separate offices or roles. The Father sends the Son. The Son is submissive to the Father; he is the *incarnation* [em-*bodi*-ment] of the Father and does the Father's will rather than his own. And the Spirit proceeds from the Father and mediates the presence of the Son.

These analogies suggest that although we may not fully understand the simultaneous unity and duality of spirit and body, we should be somewhat comfortable with it because God's world is filled with similar mysteries.

These analogies also remind us to be careful not to emphasize our duality over our unity.[13] Heart and body are both two and one. They are two in that body cannot be reduced to heart or spirit, and heart cannot be reduced to body. But they are mutually interdependent. They need each other. Human life cannot even be imagined without both the inner and the outer person. Paul's discussion on the resurrection of the body follows from this. In the context of 1 Corinthians 15, the apostle cannot think of the person as one substance or the other; man is both body and soul. If there is a death of the body, there must also be a resurrection of the body in order to have eternal life.

At the level of the brain, this unity suggests that the heart or spirit will always be *represented* or *expressed* in the brain's chemical activity. When we choose good or evil, such decisions will be accompanied by changes in brain activity. When we think about how to disciple our children, there will be unique brain activity. This does not mean that the brain *causes* these decisions. It simply means that the brain ren-

---

13 Stephan Evans's use of the word "minimal dualism" is most appropriate. C. Stephan Evans, "Separable Souls: A Defense of 'Minimal Dualism,'" *Southern Journal of Philosophy* 19 (1981): 313–31.

ders the desires of the heart in a physical medium. It is as if the heart always leaves its footprints on the brain.

Knowing this, we are more prepared for research suggesting that the brain of the angry person is different from the brain of the pacifist, or that the brain of a homosexual is different from the brain of a heterosexual. Instead of denying or arguing with these observations, we would expect them: the Bible predicts that what goes on in the heart is represented physically. But the Bible would clarify that such differences do not prove that the brain *caused* the thoughts and actions. It may very well be the opposite. Brain changes may be *caused by* these *behaviors.*

Does this make you feel a little less intimidated by some of the new brain research? You may not be able to read a technical study on the brain, but you should be confident that God's Word is able to rule wisely over this sometimes rebellious discipline. In fact, God's Word still holds secrets that are rarely fathomed by those who interpret brain research. It indicates that there is something about the person that persists, even when the brain is wasting away. Secular medicine only has hints of this reality. For example, the famous Russian neuropsychologist A. R. Luria wrote, "A man does not consist of memory alone. He has feeling, will, sensibility, moral being—matters of which neuropsychology cannot speak. And it is here . . . that you may find ways to touch him, and change him."[14]

---

14 O. Sacks, *The Man Who Mistook His Wife for a Hat* (New York: Harper & Row, 1985), 34.

CHAPTER

MIND-BODY:
PRACTICAL APPLICATIONS

THEOLOGY is full of applications, and a basic theology of the body, the heart, and their interrelationship is no exception. The more you live with it, the more you see its relevance to daily questions. In this chapter we will consider four practical principles that emerge from the mind-body discussion. They are as follows:

> The brain cannot make a person sin or keep a person from following Jesus in faith and obedience.

> Each person's abilities—brain strengths and weaknesses—are unique and worthy of careful study.

> Brain problems can expose heart problems.

> Sinful hearts can lead to physical illness, and upright hearts can lead to health.

The Brain Cannot Make a Person Sin

The first practical application of a biblical view of the heart and the brain is that the brain cannot make us sin. If you said that the *body*

49

cannot make us sin, many people would agree. After all, a broken arm, acute back pain, or heart disease can be painful, but it cannot make us sin. But, for some reason, when the problem is an alleged brain problem, we often excuse sin. For example, consider this excerpt from a morning newspaper:

> A judge has dismissed a drunken driving charge against a woman who says she was suffering from premenstrual syndrome when she used vulgar language and kicked a state trooper.

Most men and women would probably agree with the judge: premenstrual syndrome (PMS) makes life more difficult, and we should give women a little slack right before their period. We might not say that this officer-assaulting woman couldn't help herself, but we might say that she probably didn't mean to do it. She was just having a bad day.

But think about this for a moment. Even if she didn't mean to do it, she is still responsible for her moral behavior: "If a person sins and does what is forbidden in any of the LORD'S commands, *even though he does not know it,* he is guilty and will be held responsible" (Lev. 5:17). Pleading ignorance to jaywalking when you didn't know there was a law against it might get you out of a ticket, but pleading ignorance to God's law doesn't work, especially since we all have "the requirements of the law written in our hearts" (Rom. 2:15).

While we certainly agree that life can be more difficult at certain times in a woman's monthly cycle, do we really want to excuse sinful behavior by blaming the brain? Notice some of the fallout of such a position. First, it takes away the privilege of turning to Jesus for power to grow through difficulties. If it is the brain's fault, the most a woman can hope for is some measure of physical healing. But if she realizes that sinful behavior flows out of the heart, she can boldly pray for power to trust and obey during her PMS days.

A second consequence of excusing sin is a political one. If PMS is to blame for sin, then a woman is declaring that she is morally handicapped at certain times of the month. By so doing, she is putting the entire women's movement in jeopardy. Forget about a woman president unless, of course, the candidate has been through menopause (assuming that menopause does not affect the brain). Forget about a woman being accepted into any position where her daily decisions have implications for others, unless there has been a medical evaluation that rules out PMS.

The biblical principle that the brain cannot make us sin may seem harsh and unsympathetic at first, but it actually is humanizing. It shows respect. It leads us to treat each other as people created in God's image. It also offers hope. True, there are some symptoms of PMS and other problems that are distinctly physical and may not improve. However, if these symptoms are accompanied by spiritual problems, then, by God's grace, we can expect that these spiritual problems will change.

A corollary of the fact that the brain cannot make us sin is this: *the brain cannot keep a person from following Jesus in faith and obedience.* Instead, the apostle Paul suggests that physical weakness is an opportunity to be spiritually *strengthened.* As 2 Corinthians 4:16 states, "Therefore we do not lose heart. Though outwardly we are wasting away, yet inwardly we are being renewed day by day."

What a delight to realize that sickness cannot rob us of faith and a dynamic knowledge of God. It gives new meaning to the fact that nothing—even brain problems—can separate us from the love of God (Rom. 8:39). By God's grace we can have strong spirits even if we have decrepit bodies. Consider, for example, a seventy-two-year-old woman who was experiencing significant intellectual changes from Alzheimer's disease. Even though she was almost mute and could not remember many of her visitors (including her own children), she remained joyful. She was gracious, kind, and patient with everyone. Her world was narrowing and she could comprehend little, but she would often remind people, "Jesus loves you" and "I love Jesus." The body and intellect were declining quickly, but her spirit seemed to soar. By God's grace, her brain "weakness" did not take away her relationship with God.

Consider too a case study from Oliver Sacks, M.D., a neurologist who writes without any apparent religious intent. He describes a man with Korsakov's syndrome, a severe brain impairment that leaves its victims with no ongoing memory.

> One tended to speak of him, instinctively, as a spiritual casualty—a "lost soul": was it possible that he had really been "desouled" by a disease? "Do you think he *has* a soul?" I once asked the Sisters. They were outraged by my question, but could see why I asked it. "Watch Jimmie in chapel," they said, "and judge for yourself."
>
> I did, and I was moved, profoundly moved and impressed, because I saw here an intensity and steadiness of attention and concentration that I had never seen before in him or conceived him capable of. I watched him kneel and take the Sacrament on his tongue, and could not doubt the fullness and totality of Communion, the perfect alignment of his spirit with the spirit of the Mass. Fully, intensely, quietly, in the quietude of absolute concentration and attention, he entered and partook of the Holy Communion. He was wholly held, absorbed, by a feeling. There was no forgetting, no Korsakov's then, nor did it seem possible or imaginable that there should be; for he was no longer at the mercy of a faulty and fallible mechanism— that of meaningless sequences and memory traces—but was absorbed in an act, an act of his whole being, which carried

feeling and meaning in an organic continuity and unity, a continuity and unity so seamless it could not permit any break.[1]

There are times when brain disease or injury may be so severe that affected people seem unresponsive and unaware of their surroundings. In such cases, the person will be like a person asleep: though not separated from the love of God, he or she will not be responsive to biblical truths and encouragement. But the breadth of this principle will surprise you. If you are able to communicate the love of Jesus in language that a young child can understand, then you will be able to communicate the Gospel meaningfully to severely brain-injured people.

Each Person's Abilities—His Brain Strengths and Weaknesses—Are Unique

The second principle is a simple one: each person's abilities are unique. This may not seem very important when a person is similar to you, but when you are helping people whose abilities are different from your own, it means that you must be alert to these differences and prepared to study them.

I once met with a man who appeared teachable, yet he seemed resistant to counsel. I had asked him to read a chapter in the Bible that I was confident would be very helpful for him. Yet each time we met he confessed, with what I thought was feigned embarrassment, that he had not yet read it. I was about to stop meeting with the man when I thought I would try one more thing—we would read the chapter together. It was then that I discovered that his "obstinance" was actually something else. The man could not read.

This admittedly is an extreme case. It should have been obvious to me early on that this man avoided written material, but I never really

1 O. Sacks, *The Man Who Mistook His Wife for a Hat* (New York: Harper & Row, 1985), 37–38.

took the time to understand his particular strengths and weaknesses. With some people, we can get away with such an oversight because their brain abilities are similar to our own. There are other people, like children or the mentally retarded, with whom we instinctively adjust to their particular strengths and weaknesses by simplifying our vocabulary. Yet there are others whose cognitive strengths and weaknesses are less obvious. In these cases we must be more diligent to study them.

A classic case would be a boy whose learning abilities are different from the rest of his siblings. On routine inspection, his parents observe that all their children are able to read and write, and their oral language abilities are above average. When the boy's older siblings all do well in school, the parents assume that this youngest son will follow in their footsteps. Yet his grades never measure up to the family average. Laziness? Attention-getting? Indifference? These all may be true, but the parents must first study their child's cognitive strengths and weaknesses.

Educational testing is one way to get some of this information, but a good observer can learn quite a bit just by looking over the boy's shoulder as he does his schoolwork. Possible weaknesses could include some of the following:

➤ He can't see the blackboard.

➤ He can write down a homework assignment when he sees it written on the blackboard but not when he hears it.

➤ He gets distracted easily.

➤ He has trouble with subtraction but not addition.

➤ He forgets to bring his books home.

➤ He is simply less intellectually able than his siblings.

➤ He has a hard time keeping directions in the right order.

Any of these facts could be gleaned by an attentive observer, and each one could be addressed in a specific way. The point is this: each person has a unique assortment of cognitive gifts and weaknesses. The more that package of abilities is different from your own, the more you will have to study the other person.

This common-sense principle is assumed in Scripture. For example, when God says "work," he doesn't say that everyone must produce two tents daily. No, he simply implores us to work "unto the Lord," to the best of our abilities (see e.g., Matt. 25:14–30; Luke 12:47–48; Eph. 6:7). Although we never minimize or excuse sinful behavior, we treat people with one talent as if they have one talent, those with five as if they have five. We treat people according to their abilities. We approach an uneducated child differently than an educated and experienced adult, a mentally gifted child differently than one who is developmentally delayed. One child may get all C's on a report card, and it will be time to celebrate. Another child may get all C's, and it will be time to curtail outside activities.

This principle is also relevant with those we consider to have normal brain functioning. For example, aren't some marital difficulties a result of assuming that your mate's cognitive abilities are identical to your own? If you can balance the checkbook, then everyone should be able to balance one. If you are able to estimate exactly how much time you need to shower and get dressed, then everyone else should be accurate in their estimates as well. If you are mentally alert and ready to talk at midnight, then so should your mate. All of these problems arise when spouses are unwilling to study the particular strengths and weaknesses of their partners.

This principle is also relevant when there has been sinful behavior. Sin is clearly an expression of the heart, and brain weaknesses are never an excuse for sin, but brain weaknesses do influence the person. Therefore, if you are living with an angry, demented father whose abusive speech gets the entire house in an uproar, you don't immediately say, "Dad must be rebuked for his sin." Instead, you try to understand what he understands. In so doing, you might recognize that he feels out of control and helpless. Perhaps he thought that you were trying to poison him or hold him hostage. If this is his inner world, anger might have been an appropriate response. How would you help him then? You might assure him of your love and care, give him opportunities to go for walks by himself (with someone watching close by), or change the subject either to a topic that interests him or to one about which he feels more confident. Certainly the expression of his grief and confusion by way of abusive anger is sinful, but a wise friend takes into account the larger situation.

Would you call your father to repent? The rule of thumb is that if someone is able to be verbally or physically abusive, he or she is able to understand that the behavior is wrong. This does not mean that calling a brain-altered person to repentance is easy. You may have to seek counsel from those who have experienced similar problems in order to communicate effectively.

This also does not mean that you must immediately call a person to repent for every biblical infraction. For example, when my children were younger and were up late, they tended to be impatient, slow to obey, and full of complaints. Their behavior was wrong. But their goal was not blatant rebelliousness—they were exhausted! Instead of disciplining them, my wife and I would send them to bed. Then the next day we reminded them that God can help them to have self-control when they are tired.

Brain Problems Can Expose Heart Problems

This last illustration raises another important principle. When my children were tired, it was probably not the best time to discipline them. But their tiredness allowed me to see something important. It allowed me to see their hearts. Problems with the brain or body can expose what is in our hearts.

You can see this principle at work in a person with Alzheimer's disease, a man who was once considered godly but now makes lewd remarks to women and is sinfully demanding of those who are close to him. What about the man diagnosed with bipolar disorder who was adulterous while in a manic phase? Or what about the person who seems courteous and mild-mannered when sober but is vulgar and belligerent when drinking alcohol? In these situations it appears that the brain led the person into sin, yet it would be more accurate to say that their brain problems allowed their sin to be revealed.

Here is an analogy. Let's assume that you have a spouse who criticizes one of your idiosyncrasies, such as the way you blow your nose. Such occasional criticism may be bothersome, but you overlook the insult. If, however, your spouse persists in these comments, or becomes increasingly critical about what you do, then overlooking the insult is not so easy. Perhaps, if you are having a good day, you graciously confront your spouse, but chances are that you will start throwing back a few zingers of your own. *Your* sense of justice demands that your spouse's criticism be judged with your own critical and sarcastic remarks. After all, you are not a doormat—it just seems fair.

But seeming fair and being right are two different things. The right thing to do is to confront your spouse in love, repay evil with good, or perhaps ask a mutual friend to help mediate. Although it feels natural to fight your spouse's criticism with increasingly virulent criticism of your own, the reason you are responding this way is because of your own heart. You are attacking rather than loving. Furthermore, you can't say, "My spouse made me do it." Your spouse was the *occasion* for your sin. He or she became the opportunity for your sin to be revealed or exposed. That other person has *tested* your heart or been a stumbling block, but that person is not the cause for your own sin. Instead of *cre-*

ating your anger, your spouse simply *exposed* tendencies that were already in your heart. It just took the right circumstances to bring the issues in your heart to the surface.

In a similar way, a person whose brain has been altered by disease or drugs cannot excuse sin by saying that the brain or the drugs "made me do it." A dysfunctional brain can make it very difficult to understand what is going on, but it can't create sin. It can only reveal things that were previously hidden in the heart. And the reason these things were *hidden* was that circumstances were never intense enough to expose them (we tend to see our hearts when trials are intense), or the person had the mental self-control just to *think* something but not actually say it.

Therefore, the person with Alzheimer's disease, the person diagnosed with mania, and the heavy drinker all had brain problems that exposed the thoughts and intents of the heart. The man with Alzheimer's had a lifestyle of looking good on the surface but of indulging himself with sexual thoughts in his private world. The man who became sexually active during manic phases found that his mania provided two things: it gave him boldness to pursue his desires, and it made him less aware of the opinions of others. And the person whose behavior changed while intoxicated was only revealing himself. In some cases, brain problems function like truth serum for the heart.[2]

Sinful Hearts Can Lead to Physical Illness; Upright Hearts Can Lead to Health

A fourth principle that proceeds from a mind-body theology is perhaps the most familiar. It is often referred to as psychosomatic prob-

---

2 It is not only brains and spouses that can reveal our hearts. They are only a sample of hundreds of influences that can have similar effects. These influences include living with alcoholic parents, bad weather, poverty, prosperity, friends, and teachers. Even Satan is included.

lems. The common secular conception of these problems is that stress alters the body's susceptibility to diseases. The theory is that when we are struggling to cope with problems in marriage, relationships, or work, the body gradually loses its ability to fight disease. With this we would all agree. What goes on in our hearts can have physical consequences.

The Christian view has points in common with the secular view of psychosomatics, but it is distinctive in important ways. First, it suggests that what we call stress is not always an expression of the heart. Living in a world that is fallen and under the curse is simply difficult. Work is hard and there are many demands on our time. This can lead to what we call stress, but it does not necessarily come from the heart. Second, if stress-related physical problems *are* from the inner person, the biblical view indicates that stress is from sinful choices or unwise living. Sin, unwise living, and guilt can lead to sickness; righteousness and the peace and joy of biblical living can lead to health.

There are a number of biblical references that illustrate this connection.

Honor your father and your mother, so that you may live long in the land the LORD your God is giving you. (Exod. 20:12)

If you pay attention to these laws and are careful to follow them, then the LORD your God will keep his covenant of love with you. . . . The LORD will keep you free from every disease. He will not inflict on you the horrible diseases you knew in Egypt, but he will inflict them on all who hate you. (Deut. 7:12, 15)

[Because of the wickedness of Jehoram king of Judah] the LORD afflicted Jehoram with an incurable disease of the bowels. In the course of time, at the end of the second year, his bowels came out

because of the disease, and he died in great pain. (2 Chron. 21:18–19)

Because of your wrath there is no health in my body;
    my bones have no soundness because of my sin.
My guilt has overwhelmed me
    like a burden too heavy to bear.
My wounds fester and are loathsome
    because of my sinful folly. (Ps. 38:3–5; see also Ps. 32).

. . . fear the LORD *and shun evil.*
This will bring health to your body
    and nourishment to your bones. (Prov. 3:7–8)

These verses suggest that *some* physical problems have spiritual causes. Chronic pain, the physical symptoms of depression, psychiatric problems, and a host of other medical symptoms might qualify. How can you know if sin did it? You can't. Usually, instead of giving us the clear cause for a sickness, the Bible simplifies the problem by saying that those who are sick, whatever the cause, need prayer and encouragement from others. Furthermore, sickness is an opportunity to grow in repentance, faith, and obedience. The only time you have reason to suspect a connection between sin and sickness is when repentance and faith are followed by physical healing. Even then, however, there may have been other reasons for the alleviation of the symptoms.

The psycho- or spiritual-somatic connection is not an unbending rule. Our sins do not always lead to physical disability, and our faithfulness does not always lead to health. Instead, God is gracious to sinners, protecting them from the physical consequences that their sins deserve. And he is gracious to those who are obedient and faithful, allowing them to experience physical problems as a way to keep them from getting too settled in any place other than heaven.

THESE four principles should be a sufficient biblical foundation for understanding brain-related problems. They may seem theologically very ordinary—and they *are* ordinary—but they are sufficient. All we have done is reaffirm Scripture's teaching that we are a unity of material and immaterial substance, spirit and body. But in the history of this discussion, there has been something lacking. There has been very little application. In God's providence, there have been questions raised in this generation that force us to think more practically about this basic theology. These four principles are the practical application. Now let's see how they work.

PART TWO *Brain Problems*
Seen Through the
Lens of Scripture

Part Two examines three areas where Scripture is especially interested in overseeing the brain sciences: brain diseases that affect behavior, psychiatric problems, and behaviors that were once called sin but are now considered either sickness or normal. These three areas raise questions about personal responsibility and spiritual responsiveness, and they are in need of biblical adjustments. But biblical adjustments are not the only reason for Scripture's special interest. These three areas are also about people—people who are struggling, people who are suffering, people who need the ministry of the church. And Scripture, applied by the Holy Spirit, can mobilize the church for this task.

Chapters 4 and 5 are titled "The Brain Did It." These chapters will show you how to biblically understand and care for those who have real diseases that affect brain functioning. There are scores of known diseases and dysfunctions of the brain that affect mood, intellect, and behavior, and time does not permit us to look at them all. Instead, chapters 4 and 5 will generate principles that can be applied to them all by examining two of the most common problems: dementia associated with Alzheimer's disease and head injury from accidents. My goal is to provide you with a *method* for approaching physical problems and gaining experience in distinguishing issues of the heart from physical weakness.

Chapters 6 and 7 are titled "*Maybe* the Brain Did It." These chapters consider the ever-expanding world of modern psychiatry. They present some of the strengths and weaknesses of their diagnostic system, and they show how the Bible stands "over" these diagnoses. This section will explain principles that are relevant to most psychiatric diagnoses by examining two common problems: depression and attention deficit disorder.

Chapters 8 and 9 are titled "The Brain *Didn't* Do It." These chapters consider another expanding category: behaviors that were once thought sinful but are now assumed to be either normal or the result of disease. The classic illustrations are homosexuality and alcoholism, and these two issues will be our focus. They are, however, only among the better known problems. Also included in this category are anger, fear, and anything that can loosely fit into the category of addiction.

The Brain Did It:
Brain Dysfunction

ALZHEIMER'S DISEASE AND DEMENTIA

WHEN Sue's father came to live with her family, she had no idea that it would be harder for her than it would be for him. After all, he was the one with Alzheimer's disease.

But every other day she is in tears, wondering how her father could be so insensitive. He calls her three or four times throughout the night, every night. Sometimes he asks for, or demands, a glass of water when one is sitting on the night stand. Sometimes he asks for breakfast at 3:00 A.M. Sometimes he asks what time it is, or accuses her of trying to kill him, or complains about the bed, or sits and cries for no apparent reason.

Sue thought that having her father live with them, even though he had been diagnosed with Alzheimer's, would be good for her children. So far, however, she has been wrong. At his best, her father has ignored the children. Usually, he acts as if they are a nuisance. Sometimes he uses crude language and makes sexual comments in front of them. As a result, the children do everything they can to avoid him. They have started spending more time at the homes of friends, and they are embarrassed to bring anyone home.

Sue's husband has been supportive and helpful. He pitches in where he can, but his patience is growing thin.

It is starting to get to her, too. But Sue's style is to get down on herself rather than her father. For example, she hates what she sees in herself. As the months go on, she has done and thought things she never even considered before. She has been angry with her father, and so she feels guilty. She keeps trying to please her father, but he is never pleased, and so she feels guilty. There are times when she wishes her father were in a nursing home, and so she feels guilty about that too. There have even been times when she has imagined how much nicer things would be if he died, which has left her crushed by guilt.

I'm a complete failure, she silently moans. Her father is miserable, her family seems scattered, she is always tired, and she feels full of guilt. She is afraid to talk to anyone else because that will only publicize her failures. What can she do?

A place to start is to ask for help. She must turn from her pride—pride that she must always please other people and be the "do everything" wife and mother—and use the people resources that God has given her. Sue needs to remember that God graciously takes us to the end of ourselves so that we will rely on him and the resources he gives us in other people. This help should follow four basic steps (Figure 4.1).

First, she must *get information about the disease and its mental and emotional consequences.* She must consult an attentive, knowledgeable physician, and she, along with the family, should read whatever is available about the disease. Too often families prefer denial over education. Denial lets families believe the myth that all is well, and it keeps people from confronting the bitter reality of the physical decline and death of a loved one. But these perceived benefits come at a high cost. The dementing adult is already confused. The lack of information and frank discussion only make it worse. Family and friends are frustrated by the person's behavior, yet their ignorance keeps them from finding

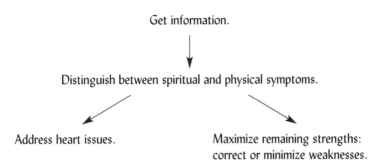

Figure 4.1. Steps for helping those with brain problems

solutions. Meanwhile, children are perplexed or embarrassed by the strange behavior that may accompany brain-altering diseases. Reading current literature can prepare families, and it will provide an opportunity to understand the inner world of affected persons.

Second, Sue must be able to *distinguish between physical symptoms and spiritual problems.* Since we approach physical and spiritual problems in different ways, we need to be able to distinguish between them. Physical problems are met with understanding, compassion, and creative teaching. Spiritual problems are also met with understanding, compassion, and creative teaching, but the content of the teaching is the law of God and the Gospel of Jesus, and the response is repentance and faith rather than intellectual understanding or simple behavioral change. Sue needs to ask this question when she deals with her father's behavior: Does this behavior violate God's commands, is it a result of brain changes, or is it both?

Third, Sue must creatively *address the heart.* Keep in mind that brain disability does not mean spiritual disability. Even in the more severe forms of brain injury and deterioration, there remains a conscience, an ability to respond to God, and an ability to turn from sin. The challenge is to communicate God's truth in a way that is understandable and memorable.

Fourth, Sue can *maximize remaining strengths (and, if necessary, teach skills to minimize weaknesses)*. We treat dementing people in the same way we would anybody: we want to understand and encourage their gifts or strengths. Sometimes we might have to teach skills to compensate for their weaknesses, but our focus should be more on their strengths.

What are their strengths, gifts, and abilities? What do they enjoy doing? Often it is easier to do things yourself, but there are times when you should choose the harder path if it means giving the demented an opportunity to serve. Do you ask them for prayer? Do you ever seek their advice? When they use their remaining gifts, God blesses them and they can bless others.

What Is Alzheimer's Disease and Dementia?

The aging of America has made dementia a critical issue confronting both the church and society at large. Medical care, housing, responsibilities of the spouse and children, ways to honor dementing adults, role reversals—these are just a few of the potentially overwhelming problems that must be addressed by the caring community. The situation, however, is far from despairing. With education about the disease, solid biblical principles, a good diaconal team, and a family committed to ministry, the care of a dementing adult can be an edifying experience for an entire church.

Dementia has taken the place that *senility* once had in our vocabulary, and for good reasons. *Senility* carried too much excess baggage—it had derogatory connotations and it tended to be associated with the myth that all older people became senile. It is still used today, but it has a more limited meaning. *Senile* simply refers to age sixty-five and older. Therefore, a presenile dementia is one that emerges before age sixty-five, and a senile dementia occurs at or after age sixty-five.

Dementia is *not* an inevitable consequence of aging. It is easily distinguished from the dulled senses and occasional forgetfulness of old age. Actually, it is a fairly generic term that refers to a deterioration of memory and intellect severe enough to interfere with social relationships and work. It may be brief and reversible, as in an alcoholic stupor or a severe hypoglycemic episode, or it may be chronic and progressive, as in the most well known of dementias—Alzheimer's disease.

Alzheimer's disease (AD) is an increasingly common dementia that can strike surprisingly early, even as soon as the early forties. The fourth leading cause of death in the U.S., AD affects about 1 percent of the population under age sixty-five and its statistics rise dramatically to include about 20 percent of the population over eighty. Its penchant for older adults is especially significant because those who are eighty-five and older represent the fastest-growing age group in our population.

The changes most commonly associated with Alzheimer's disease occur in the nerve cells of the cerebral cortex. Under an electron microscope, accumulations of abnormal nerve fibers appear as chaotic, tangled filaments. These were first described in 1906 by a German neurologist, Alois Alzheimer.

What you may find surprising regarding Alzheimer's disease is that definitive medical tests that can diagnose it are still in their infancy. One promising and simple test suggests that the neurochemical acetylcholine may be deficient. To test for this, a drop of medicine is used to dilate the pupil. In AD patients, the degree and duration of pupil dilation is much greater than in unaffected patients. Other promising tests are on the horizon, but none is yet highly reliable. As such, the first agenda with those who demonstrate intellectual decline is a comprehensive medical work-up to rule out the host of diseases that can mimic Alzheimer's.

Known Treatable Dementías

Since diagnosis is not a clear-cut process, many people have been misdiagnosed as having AD when there was actually a treatable underlying problem. It has been estimated that up to one-fourth of those originally diagnosed with Alzheimer's do not have the disease! For them, their families, and friends, misdiagnosis is a tragic error.

The most frequent imitators of AD are depression and the side effects of prescription drugs—both very treatable. Depression is easily misdiagnosed because, along with the difficult emotions, it is accompanied by dementia-like mental and physical sluggishness. In fact, mental and physical slowing may be the most prominent symptoms of depression—even more pronounced than complaints of feeling depressed. (Many older people would rather admit to physical problems than emotional.) For the family, this means that evidence of intellectual changes in the elderly must be accompanied by both a thorough medical evaluation and a systematic counseling interview. "Have there been any recent changes in your life? Death of loved ones? Physical disability? A sense of purposelessness? What have these changes been like for you?" "Have you been feeling depressed recently?" If you note any evidence of depression, be sure to alert those who are considering the diagnosis of Alzheimer's.

The other major offender, prescription drugs, is notorious for causing dementia. Yet even though almost everyone is aware of the potential problems of multiple medications in the elderly, drugs are still casually prescribed for even minor complaints.

For example, Mr. Lee, at age fifty-two, began to experience episodic confusion and intellectual decline. He was treated with medication and diagnosed with Alzheimer's disease. The medical community suggested nursing home care because Mr. Lee seemed unable to care for himself. For nine years he and his family lived under the

Alzheimer's shroud. Finally, the family funds depleted, Mrs. Lee brought her husband home and chose to cut off all his medication. After suffering some withdrawal symptoms, Mr. Lee improved dramatically. He recovered, largely a result of the resilience of his relative youth. Amazingly, he went on to teach college math.

The scenario goes like this. Older people are already taking medication for chronic illnesses. Then, when they experience drug-related fatigue, depression, mild memory problems, or sleep loss, they are often prescribed more medication. Not infrequently, this medication will have side effects, so it is deemed necessary to prescribe more medication again. Perhaps a young adult can withstand this chemical deluge, but older persons, with their more fragile metabolism and fatigued kidney and liver function, are slow to excrete the drugs. The gradual accumulation of psychoactive drugs can then produce a downward intellectual spiral that mimics the untreatable Alzheimer's.

One way to prevent this form of dementia is to keep a list of every drug an elderly person is taking. Then, make certain that *every* physician involved in the medical treatment is aware of the drug list. Also, know *why* someone is taking drugs and *how much* they are supposed to take. Ask questions of the primary physician if you suspect that the prescriptions are unnecessary. And remember that second opinions are standard in American medicine.

Depression and the side effects of medication are not the only treatable causes of dementia. Table 4.1 lists *some* of the treatable dementias simply to remind you that intellectual decline in the elderly does not necessarily mean AD or another untreatable dementia.

If you are aware of subtle intellectual changes in a family member, get a doctor who will listen, answer questions, and, if warranted, pursue a series of medical and intellectual tests. These tests may include the following: chest X-ray, skull CT scan, EKG, EEG, urinalysis, stool testing, liver function tests, thyroid function tests, arterial blood gases,

Table 4.1 Some Known Treatable Dementias

Toxins and Drugs	**Trauma**
Prescription and over-the-counter drugs	Subdural hematoma
	Heat stroke and hypothermia
Street drugs	
Alcohol	**Vascular disease**
Toxic substances encountered at work	Stroke
	Multi-infarct dementia
Infections	**Deficiency states**
Brain abscess	Pellagra (niacin)
Meningitis (bacterial or fungal)	Vitamin B-12 deficiency
Mononucleosis	Wernicke-Korsakov's syndrome
	Anemia
Endocrine and metabolic disorders	Marchiafava-Bignami disease
Thyroid disorders (myxedema, Grave's disease)	
	Other diseases
Parathyroid disorders	Brain tumor
Liver disease	Normal Pressure Hydrocephalus
Wilson's disease	Whipple's disease
Cushing's syndrome	Fever
Renal failure, uremia	Depression
Respiratory failure	Dehydration
Hyperglycemia and hypoglycemia	Hearing aid dysfunction

electrolytes (sodium, potassium, calcium, magnesium), basic blood tests, CSF exam, fasting blood sugar, vitamin deficiencies, and review of current medications. Most work-ups will also include an evaluation of memory and intellectual function.

The Course of Alzheimer's Disease

The course of AD is progressive, but its pace is unpredictable. It can last anywhere from three to fifteen years or more. Its incessant onslaught is not prone to plateaus, and yet some families experience different stages of the disease.

The Early Stage

The onset of Alzheimer's disease is usually insidious. It may begin as "forgetfulness," apparent only to fellow workers or a spouse. What makes it even more difficult to detect initially is that workers may cover up for the dementing adult, and families are quick to deny any significant changes. One son put it this way:

> Over the period that we worked together, I became gradually aware that the fine edge of his intellect was becoming dull. He was less clear in discussion and less quick to make the fine jump from a new piece of evidence to its possible significance. He spent more time over his work and achieved less; and he found it increasingly difficult to get his work ready for publication. He tended to become portentous and solemn about his subject, as though one small corner of knowledge nearly filled his world and the wider horizons were narrowing in. The change was so slow as to be barely perceptible, and the signs vanish when I try to pin them down: they were like those faint stars which are seen more easily when they are not in the direct line of vision. I was left with a feeling of uneasiness which I could not justify.[1]

This early stage, lasting two to three years, is characterized by progressive changes in memory, decreased intellectual efficiency, and spatial disorientation (that is, those affected may get lost or be uncertain in previously familiar surroundings). Then, as they become overwhelmed with tasks that were once easily manageable, they may begin to withdraw in an attempt to cope with a confusing world.

1 Anonymous, "Death of a Mind: A Study in Disintegration," *Lancet* 1 (1950): 1012–15.

After a diagnosis of AD, families tend to immediately view changes once considered eccentric or humorous as signs of AD. Now, instead of bounced checks being "forgetfulness," families interpret them as harbingers of rapid cognitive deterioration. The first inclination is to relieve those with AD of any such responsibilities. Caregivers, however, must constantly maintain a goal of maximizing the person's spiritual gifts and physical abilities, and AD patients must be given as much say as possible in their care.

The key biblical principle is to honor the elderly. Honor them by listening, asking for their opinions and counsel, understanding their perspectives, helping them maintain relationships with friends, being honest with them, and working creatively to serve them. Also, within safe boundaries, give them decision-making responsibilities and ongoing ministry.

One of the most difficult decisions during this time concerns driving privileges. This is one reason why Sue's father was angry. For many adults, to rescind this is to rob them of freedom, and they may respond with anger along with absolutely brilliant strategies to get the car. Some families actually dismantle parts of the engine whenever they are not using the car. Most of this can be avoided if families get counsel from others, offer specific facts that indicate a poor driving record, and look for transportation alternatives.

Financial management poses another problem. If the person with AD is the financial manager, a spouse or relative will gradually have to perform that function. Paying bills, balancing checkbooks, locating important financial documents, and reviewing wills are all part of this financial package. At this stage, legal advice is helpful.

Later in this stage, intellectual decline becomes more obvious. For example, an adult may have difficulties recognizing and interpreting previously familiar objects, such as a shower head. As a result, a simple shower may be misinterpreted as a rain storm and the person may belligerently seek to escape to a safe place. Self-care is increasingly difficult, and the person soon needs full-time supervision. The family can minimize difficulties by establishing a structured daily routine.

For the family, perhaps the most difficult part of this stage is the patient's emotional unpredictability. Emotions can fluctuate from anger, suspicion, depression, and transient crying episodes to silliness and childish elation, all without a moment's notice. Family members are alternately perplexed, angry, and guilt-laden as they are swayed by these emotional turnabouts. This is often when families realize their need to be educated about dementia and AD. During this time, families should be reading everything they can about Alzheimer's.[2] With the help of good available literature, local support groups, and biblical studies on the elderly and honoring parents, both parents and children can be in a position to understand the strange behavior associated with AD and to grow in faith.

At this point, if not earlier, families must begin to develop resources to help them care for their parent. The self-sufficient hero role can be physically debilitating. Even more, it is biblically unsound. Families must begin looking toward other family members, the church, and perhaps community resources for assistance. The church's participation can be invaluable. Along with providing encouragement

---

2 The following books may be helpful: Donna Cohen and Carl Eisdorfer, *The Loss of Self: A Family Resource for the Care of Alzheimer's Disease and Related Disorders* (New York: Norton, 1986); this includes a fairly extensive bibliography. *Understanding Alzheimer's Disease: What Is It? How to Cope With It, and Future Directions* (The Alzheimer's Disease and Related Disorders Association, 70 East Lake Street, Chicago, IL 60601). Nancy L. Mace and Peter V. Rabins, *The Thirty-Six Hour Day: A Family Guide to Caring for People with Alzheimer's Disease, Related Dementing Illnesses and Memory Loss in Later Life,* rev. ed. (Baltimore: Johns Hopkins University Press, 1991).

and counsel, deacons and friends can provide supervision during nights or weekends away.

Other siblings and relatives are the most obvious first choice for help, but be prepared for potential problems. AD can be an opportunity for old family problems to emerge. Care for the dementing parent can resurrect old jealousies, sibling rivalries, and struggles for control. But, if possible, the AD patient could spend a few weeks each year with other family members. Granted, this can be disruptive to the older person's routine, but it provides an opportunity for him or her to spend time with other family members. It also gives the host family a break. If this is impossible, the church diaconal team and community day care centers may have to function in place of the absent or disinterested extended family.

The Middle Stage

As the disease progresses, affected individuals seem to regress; they become like dependent children. They avoid anything but a towel bath, personal toilet care is inadequate, incontinence becomes a burden on the family, emotional outbursts—occasionally precipitated by hallucinations—are frequent. Fortunately, by this time, denial and intellectual incompetence protect affected individuals from a full awareness of their problem. Families, however, don't have this recourse. Instead, they may wrongly but understandably choose to let emotional ties die and distance themselves from the patient.

Since the dementing person is less alert to his or her surroundings, including the opinions of others, it is not unusual to see unprecedented sinful behavior at this time. Does the disease create the sinful behavior? Definitely not. Is the sinful behavior a reaction to a body that is wasting away? Is the person enraged by the effects of the curse? Perhaps. More often the sinful behavior is the person's heart being revealed. Whatever the person thought or did in private is now public, because the person does not distinguish between the two any longer.

This is certainly a sobering thought. What would it be like to have our private lives broadcast to our family or friends? Sexual thoughts, jealousy, private profanity, and anger can be neatly covered when our minds are intact. But when we are intellectually less competent, some of these private events begin to slip out. It is enough to provoke us to more wholehearted obedience to Christ even though this is not the best motivation.

Along with the increased exposure of the secret ways of the heart, a curious problem in this stage is sleep disturbances. It is as if the biological day-night rhythms of affected patients parallel the confusion of their intellect. These adults may stay up all night, despite the pleas of their caregivers, and sleep in their favorite chair during the day. A variation of this is called "sundowning," in which demented persons may show very little confusion during the day, but at night, when the sun goes down, they become confused, agitated, and difficult to manage. Some of these changes may be treatable and caregivers should consult with the primary physician. Causes for sundowning include medication, pain, urinary tract problems, depression, caffeine, and frequent daily naps. Along with treating these causes, exercise and night lights are often helpful.

At this time, often after episodes of frightening, irrational behavior, many families feel unable to deal with any further decline, and they will consider nursing home placements. In addition to consulting the pastor and others regarding a nursing home decision, families should speak with the primary physician. If the patient's behavior is blatantly out of control, some physicians suggest psychoactive drugs—specifically an antipsychotic drug. These drugs can subdue some of the more difficult symptoms, but they must be used with caution as they can dull the remaining alertness of the individual.

Chapter Four

The Late Stage

At this point dementing adults produce very few comprehensible words, have difficulty walking and coordinating movements, and may not appear to recognize family members. They may seem so far removed from reality that families may think that times of talking and touching are inconsequential. Human contact, however, is important and meaningful. Families need to be reminded that although their ministry seems unappreciated, it has both temporal and eternal significance.

How to Help

This is the type of information Sue began reading on Alzheimer's disease. Whenever she found anything helpful, she shared it with her family, including her father. The increased openness was helpful for him, and the information was especially helpful for the children.

As Sue began to understand her father's world, her frustration was replaced by compassion. She realized that he was away from old friends. She especially began to understand how difficult it was for him to lose his independence. And she saw that some of his frustration was a result of living in a world that was confusing and unpredictable.

When he was frustrated, Sue would try to show honor to her dad by asking him to tell stories from his teenage years. Sometimes, when he was being particularly obstinate, she would distract him by changing the subject to something more positive. Usually this would quickly change his demeanor and, when the topic became stories from the past, the children became particularly interested.

At night, she left a night light on in his room, and she would leave the curtain partly open so that he could see what time of day it was. She also purchased a digital clock that he could see without his glasses. These steps cut down on some of the night-time calls. Her pastor suggested that she let her father know that it was very difficult for her to get up with him throughout the night, and she simply asked him if he would not call her so often. They even began to pray together that he would sleep longer and not disrupt the house when he woke.

His calls gradually became less frequent.

An unexpected result of her father's presence was that Sue saw many things in her own heart. She realized that she was quick to help but slow to ask for help. She saw that it was critical to her that other people be pleased with her. She saw that she did everything she could to avoid conflict. In the past she thought that these qualities were just part of being a Christian. Now she saw that they came out of her concern for herself.

Yet this assessment of her own heart did not leave her overwhelmed with guilt. Accompanying these revelations about her own heart were deeper insights into God's grace: his grace for help in time of need, and grace that thoroughly forgives. Such insights caused her to be quick to ask forgiveness of her father when she sinned against him. It also gave her the freedom to speak with him about his own sinful speech or actions.

With gentleness and clarity, she began to tell her father that certain behaviors were wrong. Of course, she did not point out every sin to him. But she soon spoke out against his lewd language and sexual comments. At first, she spent time trying to understand why he spoke in those ways, and occasionally she had insights that helped. Usually, however, she realized that this was simply her father's heart being exposed and she would rebuke him. When she rebuked him in love, she was usually surprised at how responsive and apologetic he became.

Certainly, Sue's life is not easy. She still gets dead tired. She still gets frustrated. And it has been painful to see her father deteriorate. But she would always say, even on the worst days, that her father's presence has been a blessing to her and her family.

An advantage that Sue has over other caregivers is that her father has made a profession of faith in Christ and is responsive to God's Word. When Scripture is presented to him clearly, he will usually respond. There are many families that do not have this advantage. Mrs. M's family, at least initially, did not.

Mrs. M is seventy years old. An avowed atheist with three married children, she was widowed at age forty-seven and struggled after that with chronic depression. Her symptoms were unchanged until, at age sixty-two, she was fired from her job. Seemingly overnight, some uncharacteristic behaviors became apparent. With no previous history of anything illegal, she was arrested for shoplifting, and, strangely, she had no recollection of the event when apprehended. (Her children concluded that she must have been lying.) She also frequently lost her car in parking lots, and she was increasingly "forgetful."

At the insistence of her children she had a medical exam in which a team of doctors, with only one dissenting vote, said, "Alzheimer's disease." Not surprisingly, the children immediately rejected the majority opinion, but they couldn't help being alerted to further signs of AD. For example, their mother participated at a senior citizens center where she was consistently yet uncharacteristically angry. She would scream in others' faces, wander aimlessly, and ask for more coffee and doughnuts when she just had some, having apparently forgotten. When the center indicated that they could no longer handle her, her children accepted the diagnosis of Alzheimer's and decided that their mother would live with the oldest daughter and her family.

During this time, most people were unaware of this woman's intellectual changes because she had a few stock phrases that made her appear socially aware and friendly. But the Alzheimer's disease was relentless. She zealously guarded "her chair" and when her grandchildren came close to it, she would sometimes hit them with her cane. Auditory hallucinations were daily companions. She wandered away from the family at stores, was up at 2 A.M. with the television blaring, and always forgot to turn off the stove. To prevent her wandering outside, she had to be locked in the house with bolts on the outside of doors! But the most striking feature of her dementia was this: in spite of all her intellectual changes, she never lost her disdain for the Gospel. Her clearest words were, "I don't want your Jesus."

This continued until one day, on the way home from a church service, she seemed to come momentarily out of her stupor and said, "I need to be forgiven for what I have done to them [old friends]." The daughter and her husband seized the moment and explained the forgiveness of Jesus expressed through the Cross. Their mother not only confessed faith in Christ, but she even told others. Her ability to communicate her faith verbally did not last long because her dementia robbed her of communication skills. However, other family members who did not claim faith in Christ were amazed at the joy they found in her face and the peace in her demeanor. She became a living example of a profound spiritual truth: "Though outwardly we are wasting away, yet inwardly we are being renewed day by day" (2 Cor. 4:16).

CHAPTER 5

HEAD INJURY

OF all the brain disabilities, perhaps no other affects individuals and families as tragically as severe head injuries. Alzheimer's disease is certainly tragic, but since it affects older people, we sometimes think it is part of the wasting-away process that we all experience. Head injury, however, typically strikes the young and active. When the affected person recovers bodily function, families have very high expectations for brain functioning as well. Families think that cognitive function will be as normal as the rest of the person's physical functioning. But if the head injury has been fairly severe, rarely are expectations fully met.

Jim was sixteen years old when he was in a car accident. He was comatose for nine days. When he came out of his coma, his parents were thrilled: their son was alive. They knew that the road back to health would be difficult, but they looked forward to Jim graduating with his high school class.

After thirty-six days in the regional medical center, Jim returned home. He was having problems with his attention and memory, and he seemed to be more impulsive and socially inappropriate, but his parents initially overlooked these problems. They assumed that these symptoms would gradually improve when he went back to school.

He returned to school two months after his accident. His friends greeted him warmly, and his family had a party for him that weekend. Things were finally getting back to normal. Yet within weeks, Jim's family and friends began to realize that he had changed. For example, he never seemed to enter into a conversation. When people were talking, he would interrupt and introduce a subject that seemed completely irrelevant. When he tried to be funny, he was just "weird." It was as if he never knew when enough was enough. It wasn't long until his friends began to avoid or ignore him.

Teachers noticed that he seemed to spend a lot of time trying to get organized for class. He was always looking for pencils or mindlessly paging through his books, apparently trying to find the right page. He seemed to understand some of the details of a class, but he rarely got the major point. Homework assignments were never submitted. He was late for classes. He was always falling asleep. And he didn't seem to care. As a result, although previously a "B" student, he was unable to keep up with his academic subjects.

When he started having fights in school, his family knew that something was not right. Jim had a temper before the accident, but he was never in fights. Now, if someone bumped him accidentally in the hallway, or if someone didn't pass him the ball on the basketball court, he would go into a rage. After a violent fight with a younger student, Jim was suspended for ten days.

When he returned, he was placed in a special education class which administered some educational and psychological tests. The tests indicated that Jim's academic skills were four years below grade level, and his emotional stability was also below the average for his age. The school decided that it would be best to place Jim in a class for the emotionally impaired. That placement, however, did nothing to improve his emotional outbursts and aggressiveness.

He started calling himself "crazy" and "dumb." After one week in this class, he tried to commit suicide by taking some pills before school. The school said that they were out of options for him.

What should the family and school do next? Like Sue and her dementing father, they needed to ask for help, and they needed to keep in mind the four steps we outlined earlier (Figure 5.1).

What Are Head Injuries?

Head injuries are not evenly distributed throughout all age groups. As you might guess, because of automobile and motorcycle accidents, they are highest among males between the ages of fifteen and twenty-five. The rates are so high, in fact, that head injuries have become one of the most common neurological disorders in the United States.

They can be broadly classified as either penetrating or closed head injuries. In penetrating injuries, an object such as a bullet penetrates the skull and brain tissue, leaving dead nerve cells in its wake. The consequences of these wounds depend on the size and location of the damage. Since they are more localized, they tend to have predictable and discrete consequences.

Closed head injuries are more common and problematic. The brain experiences fairly comprehensive damage when, after a sudden stop, it smashes into the skull, especially when it hits some bony protru-

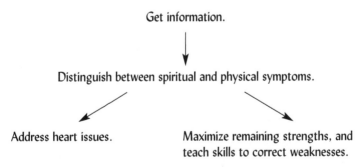

Figure 5.1. Steps for helping those with brain problems

87

sions in the frontal and temporal lobes. But the damage doesn't stop there. Since the brain is fairly soft and suspended in cerebrospinal fluid, it whiplashes or rebounds, causing further damage. Finally, the subsequent swelling or bleeding can dangerously raise the intracranial pressure and produce even further damage.

The immediate effects of closed head injuries range from being momentarily dazed to prolonged coma. Along this dimension, there are two methods of establishing severity: the Glasgow Coma Scale (GCS) and the post-traumatic amnesia (PTA). The Glasgow Coma Scale is a popular fifteen-point standardized test for assessing neurological responsiveness. It assesses eye-opening ability, physical responsiveness, and verbal responsiveness. GCS scores of 13–15 indicate a mild head injury, 9–12 moderate, and 8 or below severe. Rather than familiarizing yourself with the Coma Scale, an easier measure—and almost as helpful in establishing a prognosis—is the post-traumatic amnesia.

The PTA is the length of time between the trauma and the return of ongoing memory function. This includes a coma but is not limited to it. Patients can be responsive and seemingly alert for weeks, yet they may not remember who visited them a few hours ago or what they had for breakfast. The end of the PTA is like "waking up" to many people. Ongoing memory returns. If you are helping someone who had a severe head injury, the easiest way to determine the length of the PTA is simply by asking, "What was the first thing you remembered after the accident? When was that?"

SEVERITY OF HEAD INJURY				
HEAD INJURY	mild	moderate	severe	catastrophic
PTA	0–1 hour	1–24 hours	7+ days	months
COGNITIVE CHANGE	minor	noticeable	noticeable	permanent

Figure 5.2. Cognitive changes relative to the length of the post-traumatic amnesia

A mild head injury is characterized by a post-traumatic amnesia of less than an hour. Physical and neurological exams are typically normal in these injuries, but there is mounting evidence of more subtle nerve damage. The consequences vary. Some people experience no noticeable problems, whereas others, especially those who have intellectually demanding jobs, report chronic difficulties that emerge when they go back to work or school. Most frequent complaints include headaches, memory problems, decreased school or work performance, fatigue, dizziness, reduced concentration, insomnia, anxiety, and depression. Some people have difficulties juggling all the tasks they did before the accident. When they have to do two things at once, they feel less competent and quickly tire. Like all head injuries, obvious improvements may occur for up to two years or longer. Some people, however, report that they never make it back to their previous level of functioning.

A moderate head injury is characterized by a PTA of one to twenty-four hours. These injuries also express themselves in various ways. Some people may seem unimpaired; others may demonstrate permanent physical and cognitive changes. The accepted guideline is that when the PTA is less than twenty-four hours, a fair proportion recover intellectual and other psychological functions. If the PTA is more than twenty-four hours, persistent difficulties are the rule. Therefore, in severe brain injury, where the PTA is seven days or longer, profound, enduring cognitive changes are commonplace.

Catastrophic head injuries are accompanied by prolonged comas that can last for months. After the coma, these people typically have little interaction with or awareness of the world around them and need long-term nursing-home care. These head injuries clearly have far-reaching consequences for families, and biblical counsel and diaconal care are critical.

Cognitive and Emotional Changes After Head Injury

Although physical disabilities may exist after moderate to severe head injury, the most burdensome problems for families are the unexpected cognitive and emotional changes. Most of these changes are a result of poor concentration, poor abstract reasoning abilities, planning and organizational difficulties, changes in personality style, and changes in sexual interest (less interest or more interest). Other changes are the result of pre-existing spiritual problems being uncovered.

Most families that observe personality changes remark that the same old behaviors are present, but in an intensified, exaggerated form. Someone who struggled with lust will either do it more openly or act on it. Someone who was angry on the inside but apparently pleasant on the outside might become more openly hostile, demanding, and critical. Thus, it is not surprising that one of the best predictors of post-injury problems is pre-injury character. The cognitive impairments of those who were previously committed to biblical living will rarely lead to the same frustrating changes that are obvious in those who were not.

Secular research and case studies even support this conclusion, although, of course, they don't talk about obedience or righteousness.[1] For example, the person who was concerned about others and was responsible in work will most likely escape severe character changes after a head injury.[2] On the other hand, people who pity themselves instead of accepting and dealing more actively with their problems continue the same pattern after head injury.[3]

---

1 F. Shontz, *The Psychological Aspects of Physical Illness and Disability* (New York: Macmillan, 1975).

2 H. Kozol, "Pretraumatic Personality and Sequelae of Head Injury," *Archives of Neurology and Psychiatry* 53 (1945): 358–64.

3 M. Gruvstad, L. Kebbon, and S. Gruvstad, "Social and Psychiatric Aspects of Pre-

A forty-eight-year-old male employee was mugged on the way to make a bank deposit for his firm and was briefly unconscious. For the following twelve months, although physically and intellectually fit, he was constantly depressed and anxious, and his ability to function at work appeared to be unaccountably impaired. It was later discovered that he had a series of vocational setbacks and was now employed— in a humble job—by his successful younger brother who ran a flourishing business. It appeared that many years of resentment and hostility were now focused on the injury.[4]

A forty-five-year-old woman was disabled for many months by a number of vague complaints after surviving a car crash. The accident resulted in a minor head injury with some short-term visual problems, but there were no other injuries. Her persistent psychological complaints were curious because she seemed to deal effectively with most problems before the accident. She eventually confessed to a long-standing secret liaison with the husband of a friend, in whose company the accident had occurred. She determined to end the relationship—as penance in return for regaining her sight—and she was trying to keep her end of the bargain. It is likely that the injury became a focus for long-standing conflict and guilt.[5]

When affected by underlying sin, cognitive problems are often translated into childish behavior, unwillingness to be taught, irresponsibility, impulsiveness (especially financial), unusual emotional fluctuations, depression, and irritability. If the person goes through formal rehabilitation, he can become very angry at the "childish"

---

traumatic Personality and Post-traumatic Insufficiency Reactions in Traumatic Head Injuries," *Acta Societatis Medicorum Upsaliensis* 63 (1958): 101–13.

4 W. Lishman, "The Psychiatric Sequelae of Head Injury: A Review," *Psychological Medicine* 3 (1973): 304–18.

5 Ibid.

tasks he must perform. If these sinful responses persist, there tends to be very little progress.

Is change possible for those who tend to be impulsive, angry, and unwilling to be taught? Some improvement is likely as the injured person makes some cognitive recovery, but real hope awaits spiritual renewal. Of course, this is true for everyone, but in head injury it is particularly obvious. Remember that lack of self-awareness and poor insight into one's disabilities is common with head injuries. In such a case, an unwillingness to be taught is almost natural. After all, why would someone need to be taught when he already knew enough or was skilled enough? This is how many brain-injured people feel. They remember the skills they once had, and they assume they can do everything they could in the past. It takes great faith and wisdom for someone to be willing to be taught under such circumstances.

The head-injured person must be willing to be led by the book of Proverbs when it implores all wise people to listen and be taught by the wise.

> For lack of guidance a nation falls,
>   but many advisers make victory sure. (Prov. 11:14)

> The way of the fool seems right to him,
>   but a wise man listens to advice. (Prov. 12:15)

> Listen to advice and accept instruction,
>   and in the end you will be wise. (Prov. 19:20)

> Two are better than one,
>   because they have a good return for their work:
> If one falls down,
>   his friend can help him up. (Eccl. 4:9–10)

Like all wisdom, the only true foundation for this willingness to be taught is the fear of the Lord. If a head-injured person is willing, out of reverence to God, to receive counsel and advice, there can be hope for dramatic change. The concentration problems, the difficulties planning and organizing, the inability to do two things at once, and many other cognitive problems will probably persist, and a stable job might be dependent on an understanding employer. But when these weaknesses are no longer coupled with obvious sin, there will be dramatic improvement.

These positive changes are dependent on spiritual growth in the injured person, but they are also dependent on the spiritual quality of family and friends. As everyone in the rehabilitation field will tell you, an intact, supportive, knowledgeable, and cooperative family can make a dramatic difference.

Problems for the Family

Families, however, are inevitably unprepared for the consequences of brain injury. They typically receive little information about cognitive and behavioral changes that exist after moderate to severe brain injury. Instead, they are often told by the hospital staff that the person will "recover," and families therefore expect that, when the physical rehabilitation is over, the affected person will be back to normal in all respects. This expectation is supported by the fact that many cognitive and behavioral changes are masked in the intensive care-giving environment of hospitals. Most families never really see the psychological changes in action until the patient gets home.

This lack of information may be coupled with "faith" and "hope" that is little more than presumption and denial. Families interpret physical healing as a sign from God foretelling complete social and vocational recovery. Any contrary information is ignored. As a result, counsel is avoided and family members respond not to the changed person in front of them, but to the person they remember. It may take months and even years before families come to the end of themselves and are open to a more realistic view.

Families typically go through a series of stages when faced with brain injury. Initially they are delighted that the family member is alive, and they expect full recovery within a year. After a while, as the months begin to drag on, families begin to blame the lack of change on either themselves or the brain-injured person. Shared blame easily moves to frustration or anger with the brain-injured person. Now family expectations are lower because they perceive the patient to be "unmotivated," "irresponsible," "self-centered," or "lazy." And families often feel trapped and despairing. It is at this point that divorces are likely to occur.

These experiences can be avoided, but only with a family that is committed to understanding the affected family member and being educated in the consequences of head injury. The following suggestions are by no means exhaustive, but they offer some practical guidelines for families.

During the Hospitalization

1. Get as much information as you can. Ask questions of the primary physician; talk to the social worker; have a family conference with the rehabilitation counselor; go to the library and get information; contact community resources (e.g., local chapters of the National Head Injury Foundation). Understand the physical problems and learn of the impending cognitive and behavioral problems.

2. Decide how much time you should spend at the hospital. Round-the-clock vigils are not always wise. Yet if the family believes it is important, get someone from the church to coordinate diaconal concerns, such as meals, baby-sitting, and pet care. If the brain-injured

person remains comatose for more than a few weeks, it may be helpful to gently encourage family members to get into a more normal routine.

3. Discuss rehabilitation with the hospital staff. Since so many difficulties emerge after moderate to severe head injury, a reputable and experienced rehabilitation program is critical. This does not have to be in-patient. Programs run the gamut from long-term in-patient care to day care to in-house consultation. The follow-up needs are dependent on the resources of the family and the extent of the injury. But usually there must be some access to a multidisciplinary team trained in cognitive and behavioral changes as well as vocational rehabilitation.

The purpose of rehabilitation is to help the afflicted individual function as well as possible despite handicaps. For example, if the person has a poor memory, rehabilitation would teach memory techniques and how to function despite a poor memory. Perhaps the person would learn to make lists of names, shopping items, and so on.

In younger adults, rehabilitation is focused on vocational re-entry and job placement. It is surprising how a creative rehabilitation team and family can pinpoint abilities that can be used in the marketplace. Many victims of moderate to severe head injury can hold jobs and enjoy some measure of independence. There are, however, many individuals who never have any kind of job. Sometimes this is a result of severe cognitive deficits, but usually it is the result of cognitive deficits that are overlaid with past spiritual issues, denial, unrealistic appraisal of handicaps, fear of failure, unwillingness to take a lower position, and simple laziness.

At Home

1. Try to maintain time schedules and predictable routines. This should ease the brain-injured person's confusion and also encourage participation in home activities.

2. Realize that families are plagued by a host of emotions. Feeling trapped and isolated is not unusual. A sense of guilt is also common when families feel responsible for the lack of improvement in the affected person. Other related issues include sexual frustrations (if the head-injured person is a spouse) as a result of the head-injured person's lack of empathy and sensitivity, embarrassment, and feelings of abandonment. Families may seem like paragons of strength on the outside, but this may belie unspoken grief, frustration, and aloneness. Pastors and counselors must recognize that many families perceive their difficulties as spiritual failures and are reluctant to share their burdens with anyone. Ministry support must be able to respond without being asked.

3. Low expectations are as problematic as impossibly high ones. Families must constantly understand and help maximize patients' abilities.

4. Never allow brain injury to be an excuse for sinful behavior. When dealing with sinful behavior, recognize that there are various causes and methods to encourage change. Perhaps the family member is simply modeling and imitating the tenor of the house! The treatment, then, would be for the family to ask the affected member's forgiveness. Other sinful behaviors may be changed by simple, gentle, and loving feedback, leaving the room, or changing the subject. Don't even think about confronting the brain-injured person in anger. Sometimes family members must learn to give firm and clear comments or instructions, often with an exaggeration of gestures or tone of voice. But they must surround their interactions with the fruits of the Spirit. Finally, don't get locked into power struggles with the person. Remember that you have more mental flexibility and can see alternatives that the brain-injured cannot.

5. The brain-injured person can relearn many skills, but skills must be broken down into smaller bits of behavior, and developed

only through persistent practice. For example, a morning routine that includes showering, shaving, combing hair, and brushing teeth must be developed one step at a time. Initially, each skill will need a coach; later, after much practice, the person may be able to respond to cues such as a list in the bathroom or a series of pictures illustrating the routine.

6. When dealing with the heart, keep simple goals in mind, just as you might with children. For example, most children (like ourselves) have all sorts of problems they must work on. But a wise parent usually focuses on one or two specific issues at a time. That is not to say that the other issues are irrelevant, but they must be constantly prioritized.

7. The church should be an extension of the family. Are friends still involved socially with the family? Old friends are usually scarce within a few months of the accident. Does the family get time off if needed? Occasional meals? There are numerous gaps that can be potentially filled by the church.

8. Expect the unexpected. This doesn't mean that you avoid planning, but it does mean that at times you will have to hold onto those plans and goals lightly.

How to Help

Jim's reentry to home and school was made more difficult by a number of factors. The family was not told about the cognitive and emotional changes; there were no rehabilitation facilities in the area; Jim's teachers were unfamiliar with the consequences of head injury; and he should not have been placed in an emotionally impaired class. It was time to start over.

The parents contacted their regional head injury association for help. The association suggested an immediate conference with the parents, school principal, guidance counselor, and special education teacher. At the conference, the head injury specialist reviewed Jim's situation with the group. After giving some basic guidelines for understanding head injury, the specialist led a discussion to develop an educational plan for Jim.

They decided on the following:

1. Jim would re-enter school for the mornings only. During that time he would attend those classes in which he had been previously enrolled. He simply was unable to focus for the entire school day. Then, as he fatigued, he was more prone to emotional outbursts and fights. Shortening the school day would avoid these problems.

2. Jim would receive a duplicate set of textbooks so that he could keep one set at home. This would give him one less thing to remember and might relieve some fatigue.

3. Jim would briefly meet with a designated teacher every morning to make sure he had the right materials for the school day. At the end of the morning he would check out with the teacher to review assignments and organize projects that would take more than one night. This teacher would also coach Jim in note-taking skills.

4. Jim would have tutoring available during his morning study hall.

5. His teachers would attend a presentation about head injury. To refocus Jim when his attention was wandering, they might touch him as they walked by, or use a predetermined verbal cue that would catch Jim's attention. They would provide a written outline of the material covered, and they would check that Jim had written down all assignments. They would also try to arrange the classroom so that Jim sat near the front, away from people who could distract him. They would also give Jim more time, if needed, for tests. In some subjects, they would give him oral exams rather than written. (He could not organize his essays for written assignments.)

6. A designated student would walk with Jim to each class. This

would help Jim manage the noise and apparent confusion in the hall-ways. Like many head-injured people, he was disoriented by lots of noise and people.

The most significant problem remaining was Jim's emotional out-bursts. The school suggested that Jim meet with a professional in the community. However, now that Jim's parents better understood him, they decided to ask his youth leader if he would be willing to get in-volved.

The youth leader was happy to participate. He already had a good relationship with Jim. Prior to the accident, he had even been working with Jim on some of his frustration and impulsiveness. The youth leader was given an explanation of the cognitive changes that accom-pany head injury, yet his basic strategy for working with Jim's anger and poor self-control remained the same: they would review situations from the week when Jim had become angry and apply some basic bib-lical principles to them. They also memorized Scripture together. They studied Ephesians 4 and the book of James. And they role-played situations in which Jim had been angry.

It was especially helpful that the youth leader was around Jim in a number of social situations such as church, youth group, Sunday school, and youth group social activities. Since their relationship was a good one, the youth leader decided to give Jim feedback when he was acting weird with his peers. This was particularly apparent around the girls in the youth group. For example, Jim would initiate a conversa-tion, but he would never know when to stop. He could not understand the sometimes blatant social cues that a person wanted to leave.

Two factors shaped his social problems. First, his brain injury left him with a lack of insight into subtle social cues and the way he came across to other people. Second, some of his social problems were a re-sult of his out-of-control desires, especially his desire for a girlfriend. Jim had been watching some of his old friends spend time with girlfriends, and he had enough insight to realize that girls were not attracted to him.

The youth leader had real compassion for Jim's struggle in his desire for a girlfriend, yet he also saw the great danger. Too often *brain-injured people are unable to anticipate the consequences of their actions.* As a result, they can easily be tempted by foolishness that will provide temporary pleasure but long-term sorrow. Head-injured men are notorious for making horrible choices in relationships. Jim, even though he wanted to grow spiritually, was in danger of letting his desires rule him in this area.

What could be done? The youth leader needed to be aware of Jim's brain-based problems. For example, it was helpful for him to know that it was cognitively difficult for Jim to anticipate consequences. In other words, not only did Jim experience the normal human tendencies to live for immediate pleasure, but he also was intellectually unable to predict the consequences of his actions. This problem didn't create Jim's foolish actions, but it intensified a pattern that was already present (as it is with everyone). Knowing this, the youth leader focused on concrete, practical ways to disciple Jim in wisdom.

The youth pastor started with passages about the desires that battle within us (James 4:1–4) and explained to Jim that our idolatrous desires come out of our own pride. He also led Jim in a discussion about Proverbs 7 and its vivid picture of a foolish man and a sexually dangerous woman. All along, the youth pastor emphasized that the goal for Jim was not to get a girlfriend or just to look better on the outside. The goal was the glory of God in everything he did. This meant that they dealt with masturbation and more private thoughts of the heart.

Jim needed to grow in knowing that God was both good and great. He had to remember that God was good because he suspected that, at least in the sexual area, he knew what he needed better than God did.

He needed to know that God was great because he had to grow in reverence, fear, and worship of God. His obedience had to come out of his knowledge that God was indeed an awesome God.

Once Jim and the youth pastor had a clear direction, Jim was willing to participate in a group with five of his male peers. In this group, Jim began to share more and more of his spiritual struggles. He began to pray for the other guys, and he began to go to them for advice and counsel. Sometimes the other members of the group would get impatient and frustrated with Jim, but as they grew to know him better, they understood some of his eccentricities and no longer thought of him as head-injured.

After two years, Jim was allowed to graduate with his peers. However, he did not receive an official diploma. This allowed him to remain eligible for continuing vocational-technical education until age twenty-one. Today, he works at a local ski shop where he repairs ski equipment. He still has trouble organizing his day, but his manager, who was told about the head injury, has been willing to spend a few minutes with Jim every two hours to keep him on task.

Jim's case is one of the success stories. I share it as a way to lay out some biblical principles and to give you hope. However, if it made progress after head injury look easy, then the story has missed the mark. The story doesn't include many of the more painful experiences, such as the family's sense that they had lost their son.

Jim has been different since the accident. He responds differently to conversations; he still can seem lost when you look in his eyes. He is just not the same person. In a sense, the person the family knew before the accident is no longer with them. Therefore, you can understand why the family feels a sense of loss even though Jim is alive and at home. Three years after the accident, Jim laughed at a television show and his mother said, "I saw Jim for just a moment." Since then she has seen him more frequently.

This story doesn't include events such as the family's fear every time Jim goes out in the car. Will they get another call from the hospital telling them to come immediately?

This story doesn't describe the family's grief when they hear Jim yelling "dummy" at himself or when they hear him crying in his room.

Like most diseases or injuries that affect the brain and behavior, the disease affects the entire family, and it affects the family for years. Churches and friends must be willing to be actively involved with the family not only during the crisis, when no one knows if the affected person will live or die, but also during the difficult years that follow. Friends must be willing to *look* for ways to help (rather than ask), and they can simply ask, "How are you *really* doing?" That kind of commitment can ease the long-term responsibility of caring for a brain-injured person.

Maybe *the Brain Did It:*
Psychiatric Problems

CH A P T E R

An Introduction to
Psychiatric Problems

THIS chapter introduces problems that are typically called "psychiatric problems" or "chemical imbalances." Since these are categorically different from the obvious brain dysfunctions of Alzheimer's disease and head injury, they need some introduction.

"Psychiatric problems" refers to the dozens of diagnostic terms currently sanctioned by the American Psychiatric Association.[1] Undoubtedly, you have heard of many of them: attention deficit disorder, alcohol abuse, depression, bipolar disorder, panic disorder, anorexia and bulimia, multiple personality (now called dissociative identity disorder), and borderline personality. These are the "diseases" of this generation.

Psychiatric problems, however, are in a different class from traditional medical diseases. With most medical diseases, you can actually see what is wrong. For example, you can see a brain tumor on a CT scan, you can see the tangled neurons of Alzheimer's disease,

---

1 A list of these diagnoses can be found in *Diagnostic Criteria from DSM-IV* (Washington, D.C.: American Psychiatric Association, 1994).

and you can see the damage to the brain caused by a violent accident. Each of these conditions is clearly distinguishable from normal brains. But brain function in psychiatric problems shows no consistent differences when compared with normal brain function. Further research may reveal differences in the future, but at this time, there is no such thing as a consistent, verifiable chemical imbalance or neuroanatomical abnormality among the psychiatric diagnoses. Blood tests and brain scans are not even used in making a psychiatric diagnosis.

Does this surprise you? It probably even surprises some people who are in the medical professions. Although there are tens of thousands of research articles in this area, the careful observations of scientific research have yielded a very fuzzy picture. Unfortunately, even the areas that are somewhat clear have been complicated by the various mind-body assumptions that have been quietly providing philosophical oversight. In order to bring some clarity, let's allow Scripture to wield some influence in the discussion.

Using biblical lenses, below are three reliable propositions.

PROPOSITION 1 *Psychiatric problems are always spiritual problems and sometimes physical problems.*

This is a bold and most important assertion. You will never find a psychiatric problem where biblical counsel—counsel directed to the heart—is anything less than essential. At the very least, psychiatric problems usually indicate that the diagnosed person (and the family) is suffering in some way. And on the problem of suffering, Scripture is the expert. Through it, God offers hope, compassion, and the power to grow in faith and obedience in the midst of the suffering. For families, it provides practical guidelines on how to love and serve the person who is struggling.

But Scripture offers even more than a way to deal with suffering. Most psychiatric problems are hybrids—a combination of spiritual problems and physical ones. For example, while the hallucinations of schizophrenia may be physical, the guilt that is part of almost all schizophrenia is clearly spiritual. In these cases, not only will Scripture teach people how to live godly lives in the midst of possible ongoing hallucinations, it will deal directly with the person's guilt. And there will be some cases of schizophrenia where guilt is actually the *cause* of the physical symptoms. (Remember the "psychosomatic" principle from chapter 3?)

The myth is that psychiatric problems are strictly medical. Yet the reality is that many psychiatric problems are both physical and spiritual problems, others are thoroughly spiritual (e.g., conduct disorder in children and some of the anxiety disorders), and all of them point to difficult and sometimes painful experiences that need biblical ministry.

Too often the church, having bought the myth that these are simply physical problems, shies away from offering normal biblical counsel to those who claim a psychiatric disorder. The reason given is that these situations are too complex; they need the services of an expert who is trained in neurochemistry, neuroanatomy, and psychopharmacology. Yet the church is sitting on resources that can revolutionize treatment of these problems.

PROPOSITION 2 *Psychiatric disorders sometimes respond to medication.*

The church's reluctance to rush into the realm of psychiatric problems is with some reason. We have seen that medication might alleviate some symptoms of psychiatric disorders. Most of us know someone whose depression was tolerable only after taking antidepressant medication, or whose emotional flight of mania responded dramatically to antipsychotic medication, or whose panic attacks were relieved with antianxiety medication. The logic is that if medication can affect the symptoms, then the problem must be a chemical one, and non-medical people are not experts in chemical problems.

How are we to think about these things? Does medication really help? Is it really treating some underlying neurochemical problem? And what should our attitude be toward medication? Is it friend or foe? Since these are important questions in our culture, we would be wise to have a biblically informed perspective on them.

Does Medication Really Help?

Yes, medication can alleviate some symptoms in some people. On this there is no doubt. In some situations, medication seems to quiet the storms in the brain in a way that blesses affected individuals and their families. But that doesn't mean that you should immediately refer half the people in your church to the neighborhood psychiatrist for Prozac. The answer is not that simple. Here are some of the qualifications.

➤ There are some psychiatric problems where medication has been shown to be effective with *some* people, but medication is not effective with everyone.

➤ Many people will have adverse side effects from psychiatric medications. Some of these, such as dry mouth or weight gain, will be annoying, but the perceived benefits of the medicine will outweigh its disadvantages. Other side effects can be much more serious and the medication must be discontinued.

➤ There are potential long-term side effects associated with the antipsychotic drugs. With other psychiatric medications, some researchers have suggested that they may be ineffective or even harmful when used for a number of years. This research is difficult to interpret, so it is impossible to be definitive about the long-term effects of drugs such as the antidepressants. But it is wise to avoid medication, especially long-term medication, if possible.

➤ Too frequently, people are taking more than one medication for psychiatric problems, and there are always increased risks when taking multiple medications. In some cases, one medication is used to treat the side effects of another medication, which is used to treat the side effects of another medication, and so on.

➤ Although prescriptions for psychiatric drugs are at an all-time high, there is a growing consensus that we are being overmedicated. Since medication can be helpful *and* harmful, psychiatrists are busy getting people on medication and *off* it.

➤ Finally, there is the question, What exactly does medication help? Medication cannot change the heart: it cannot remove our tendency toward sin, it cannot revive our faith, and it cannot make us more obedient to Christ. It can, however, alleviate some of the physical symptoms associated with some psychiatric problems.

Does Medication, When Helpful, Treat Underlying Chemical Imbalances?

This question is a bit more academic, but the answer does remind us that we should not put our faith in popular interpretations of scientific research. Psychiatric medication is *not* treating a verifiable chemical imbalance in the brain. Contrary to public perception, psychiatric medications are not chemical bullets that target one particular brain chemical. They are more like chemical blitzkriegs, strafing chemical sites in the brain and hoping for the best.

The brain is simply too complex and is sustained by too many chemicals for us to be able to pinpoint chemical imbalances with our current level of knowledge. The most we can reliably say is that psychiatric medication may minimize some symptoms, but it is not necessarily treating a chemical deficiency.

Is it possible that future research will reveal confirmed chemical differences in the brains of some people with psychiatric diagnoses? According to our biblical understanding of the heart-body relationship, we would predict that one day researchers will find chemical differences. Depression, disobedience, fatigue, dyslexia, and every other human behavior is represented on a neurochemical level. This doesn't mean that the brain *causes* all these behaviors, but that the brain expresses differences in behavior at a chemical level.

Does the Bible Permit the Use of Psychiatric Medication?

If you poll people in the church, you will find a spectrum of opinions on psychiatric medication. Some will say it is from the Devil, some will say it is *the* answer, and some don't care. A more moderate opinion is that, although it is not wrong to take these medications, they are rarely our first line of attack against personal suffering. Instead, we should first consider that God can bless us through our suffering, and we might also weigh the possibility that psychiatric medications could numb us to the refining benefits of suffering.

There is a worthwhile point here. Although it may sound strange or even unloving to those who don't share a biblical position, there can be real benefits from having our faith tested and strengthened through trials.

Consider it pure joy, my brothers, whenever you face trials of many kinds, because you know that the testing of your faith develops perseverance. Perseverance must finish its work so that you may be mature and complete, not lacking anything. (James 1:2–4)

Suffering is not always something that must be escaped. In contrast to the growing American sentiment that we have a right to a pain-free existence, most everyone has personal examples of how suffering and difficulties have been essential to Christian maturity. Conversely, most everyone has witnessed the sad consequences of lives that have been artificially shielded from suffering by overprotective parents or illegal, mind-altering drugs. Given these common observations, suffering is not always the enemy that we think it is, and medication should not be considered the ultimate answer.

But there are other points to consider. First, since we don't fully know the depth of someone else's suffering, we should be careful when offering our opinion about medication. It is easy to underestimate the extent of a person's pain. Second, we should remember that, in general, the alleviation of suffering is a good thing. And third, since the Bible does not clearly prohibit these medications, the issue is not whether medication is biblically lawful or unlawful; rather, the issue is how to make wise, informed decisions.

If you are helping another person, here is a way to think about psychiatric medication. *Focus on what is clear in Scripture.* Offer the wise pastoral care outlined in Hebrews 11 and 12. It includes (1) knowing that we have been preceded by many of God's people who demonstrated strong faith in the midst of overwhelming suffering (Heb. 11), (2) ministering God's encouragement to fix our eyes on Jesus in the midst of suffering (Heb. 12:2), (3) confessing and repenting of "sin that so easily entangles" (Heb. 12:1), and (4) persevering in the suffering (Heb. 12:7).

Whether a person takes psychiatric medication or not is *not* the most important issue. Scripture is especially interested in *why* someone is taking medication or why someone is not taking medication. And it is clear that medication is never the source of our hope. With these guidelines in mind, there is biblical freedom to try, or not try, psychiatric medication.

PROPOSITION 3 *Psychiatric labels are descriptions, not explanations.*

Have you noticed that if you say, "I have attention deficit disorder [ADD]," it seems very different from saying, "It is hard for me to pay attention to verbal presentations for very long"? Somehow, the psychiatric diagnosis seems to have greater authority than the layperson's description. ADD is something you *have;* the other statement is a simple description of something you *do.* Yet the difference between the two statements is less than you think. With ADD, except for the fact that the psychiatric definition is longer, there is really no difference between the two: both describe symptoms and neither explains the cause of those symptoms.

As a description, ADD summarizes *what* a child does but not *why* he does it. The difference between the two is significant. For example, if I asked you about a car you just saw speeding by, a descriptive or "what" answer would be, "That was a green car and it was going too fast." An explanatory or "why" answer, however, would review the basics of combustion engines, the mechanics of automatic transmissions, and the motivation of the driver.

Psychiatric descriptions begin to answer *what* the child is doing, not *why.* Sometimes the descriptions can be helpful and highlight symptoms we haven't previously considered. In other words, instead of describing a green car, you might say, "That was a green Ford Taurus station wagon with a 2.0 liter engine, and it was going 73 miles per hour in a 45 mile per hour zone." This is more descriptive than saying, "A green car going too fast" (and it sounds more intelligent), but it is still just a description.

The ADD description is a careful one. If you want to understand what specific behaviors contribute to your child's poor school performance, then the symptom list associated with the term ADD might reveal behaviors that you had not previously considered. Yet this descriptive category is still limited in its usefulness.

Let's say someone asks, "Why is your son always squirming in his chair?" You respond, "Because he has ADD." This would be like saying, "He squirms in his chair because he fidgets a lot." For most people, this would not be a satisfactory answer. You are answering the *why* question with a *what* answer.

The psychiatric literature typically does not make that distinction clear. Most discussions about ADD and similar psychiatric problems assume that the lists of descriptions are equivalent to establishing a medical diagnosis—a medical *cause*. The popular assumption is that there are underlying biological causes for these behaviors, but this assumption is unfounded. Although there are dozens of biological theories to explain ADD, there are currently no physical markers for them, no medical tests that detect their presence. Food additives, birth and delivery problems, inner ear problems, and brain differences are only a few of the theories about the causes of ADD. They are all intriguing but so far unsupported by medical research. Each theory may have some merit in specific cases, but there is no one biological theory that can consistently explain the symptoms. At this point, we can't say that anyone has depression, mania, schizophrenia, or ADD in the way that someone has a virus. If we do, we are ruling out attention that must be given to the heart.

Psychiatric terms summarize a group of descriptive phrases. You would think that careful descriptions of problems would be innocent and without prejudice. But this is not the case with psychiatric vocabulary. The terms are usually loaded with assumptions of physical causes, and they do not distinguish between heart issues and physical problems. This doesn't mean that we must boycott psychiatric terminology. It simply means that we must look at it through biblical lenses. And that will be the task of the next two chapters.

CHAPTER 7

DEPRESSION

DEPRESSION has been called "a room in hell,"[1] "a howling tempest in the brain."[2] As far back as 1621, Robert Burton put his finger on it. "They are in great pain and horror of mind, distraction of soul, restlessness, full of continual fears, cares, torment, anxieties, they can neither drink, eat, nor sleep...." His description captures the experience of millions of people who struggle with depression right now.

Depression can make the most dedicated friends and ministers feel incompetent because there are times when it seems absolutely resistant to change. But depressed people are like everyone else: their inner person can be renewed by faith even in the midst of the pain. The basic steps of a biblical approach to helping them are similar to those you would follow to help people with physical problems (Figure 7.1). First, you understand the experience of depression. Second, you make tentative distinctions between physical and spiritual symptoms. Third, this distinction will allow you to focus on heart issues. In

---

1 Martha Manning, *Undercurrents* (San Francisco: Harper & Row, 1995).
2 William Styron, *Darkness Visible* (New York: Random House, 1990). Other helpful descriptions include Annie Rogers, *A Shining Affliction: A Story of Harm and Healing in Psychotherapy,* and Tracy Thompson, *The Beast: A Reckoning with Depression.*

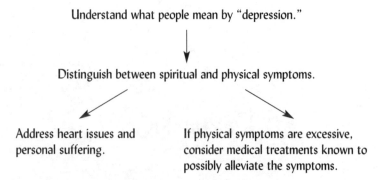

Figure 7.1. Steps to helping those who are depressed

doing this, you will point the person to Christ as her hope in suffering, you will encourage her in her faith, and you will guide her in her battle with sin. This focus on heart issues may actually relieve the depression. Fourth, if the pain of depression is excessive, consider using medical treatments to possibly ease the pain.

Understand the Experience of Depression

With traditional diseases, understanding comes from reading textbooks, consulting with those familiar with the disease, and talking with the patient. With depression, you might do all these things, but most of your understanding will come from observing and listening to the person. What is it like for him? What does she feel? What does he think?

When you listen to people describe their depression, you will hear two extremes. People will report that the pain is so intense that they want to die. Others will describe an emotional numbness in which they are already dead. Sometimes you will hear one person describe living with both extremes simultaneously.

"Pain" is the most concise description. Abraham Lincoln said, "I am now the most miserable man living. If what I feel were equally distributed to the whole human family, there would not be one cheerful face on the earth. Whether I shall ever be better, I cannot tell; I awfully forebode I shall not. To remain as I am is impossible. I must die or be better, it appears to me."

Yet the pain of depression is a curious one. Not only do people talk about the intense, palpable pain, but they also talk about being emotionally numb. J. B. Phillips in his autobiography, *The Price of Success,* writes that "the feeling of being utterly drained of all emotion and desire persisted and I simply ceased to work. . . ." Even though this seems like the opposite of pain, it is more accurately pain in another form.

A friend of mine wrote, "I am suicidal again. I have no energy or reason to fight. I am numb and tried all the things I know how to try. I know that I won't be able to function like this much longer. There is no one to talk to. I'm suffocating. I can think the best thoughts all day and I still feel like this. No one knows how badly I want to die. My thoughts are obsessive and won't stop. They keep saying, 'I want to die.' "

If depression coincides with the holidays, the pain is multiplied. "I dread holidays," a woman in the church said, "especially Christmas and Easter because they're family holidays. There is so much expectation for love and happiness. I hate holidays."

Don't assume that you understand what someone means by "depression." Don't fill in the meaning from your own experience, which may or may not be similar. Instead, listen. Allow the depressed person to fill the word *depression* with the meaning it has for him or her. When you do listen, you will hear pain, fear, hopelessness, dread of the future, terror, silent screams, and emptiness that threatens to destroy.

It even affects the senses. Sounds seem muted, music discordant. All that is left to your appreciation of music is, sadly, the memory of how much you *used to* enjoy it. Visually, colors seem less vibrant. (Do you remember the perceptual bleakness of Picasso's blue period?)

The technical description of depression is not nearly as vivid as the ones sketched out here, but it includes some symptoms that depressed people might fail to mention.

According to the *Diagnostic and Statistical Manual of the American Psychiatric Association,* 4th edition (DSM-IV), you are technically labeled depressed if you experience five or more of the following symptoms during the same two-week period. Depressed mood or loss of interest or pleasure must be one of the symptoms:

1. Depressed mood most of the day.
2. Markedly diminished interest or pleasure in all, or almost all, activities most of the day.
3. Significant weight loss when not dieting or weight gain.
4. Insomnia or hypersomnia nearly every day.
5. Feeling physically restless or slowed to an extent that is observable to others.
6. Fatigue or loss of energy nearly every day.
7. Feelings of worthlessness or excessive or inappropriate guilt.
8. Diminished ability to think or concentrate.
9. Recurrent thoughts of death, recurrent suicidal thinking without a specific plan, or an actual suicide attempt.[3]

As you begin to understand the nature of these symptoms in others, compassion is inevitable. No one can be unmoved by this inner pain.

Distinguish Between Physical and Spiritual Symptoms

The next step is to distinguish physical symptoms from spiritual ones. When you do this, you will immediately know the cause of the

3 *Diagnostic Criteria from DSM-IV* (Washington, D.C.: American Psychiatric Association, 1994), 161–64.

spiritual problems—they come from the heart, but you will not know the cause of the physical complaints. The physical complaints may be caused by a body that is wasting away, by sin in the person's life, or by Satan; or they may be a divine affliction for the purpose of teaching a person to rely on God alone.

It is important initially to distinguish between these two categories (physical and spiritual) for two reasons.

1. If we confuse physical for spiritual symptoms, we are liable to hold people morally responsible for physical symptoms.

2. If we confuse spiritual for physical symptoms, we are liable to excuse sin or have little hope for spiritual growth when someone has a psychiatric diagnosis.

To make this distinction, all you need are your two questions:

➤ Does the Bible command or prohibit this behavior?

➤ Can this behavior be best described as a strength or weakness?

Physical Symptoms

The jolting descriptions of pain are best described as physical symptoms. It certainly is not a sin to experience pain.

Emotional numbness is not so clear. Some might argue that emotional numbness is a violation of the call to rejoice in all situations. Yet I would suggest that emotional numbness is just another form of pain. People, for whatever reason, lack the physical, emotional response they once had. There is nothing morally wrong with that. Furthermore, depressed people can still be thankful and confident in God, yet have emotions that feel dead.

Other aspects of depression are more obviously classified as physical symptoms. These include sleep problems, weight changes, fatigue, and problems with concentration.

Chapter Seven

Spiritual Problems

When you read the technical description of depression, there are a few symptoms that are most likely spiritual problems. "Feelings of worthlessness or excessive or inappropriate guilt" is the most obvious. Guilt is not a sin in itself, but it is a signpost pointing to a spiritual problem. Guilt is clearly an expression of the heart and conscience. It may come from violating God's law, in which case it should be confessed. It may also come from violating personal standards, as in "I feel guilty because I did not please my spouse." This too is a spiritual problem that should not be quickly discarded as "false guilt." Guilt from the violation of false or human standards comes when we interpret the world according to our rules rather than God's. As such, false guilt, at a deeper level, is against God's Word, and it can be addressed through God's Word.

Among the technical descriptions of depression, the other symptom that might be distinctly spiritual is suicidal thinking. But we should be careful not to judge too quickly. Some thoughts of death are simply a result of wanting the pain to be over. It could actually be an expression of hope and confidence that God will wipe away every tear in eternity. Other times, suicidal thoughts can be filled with self-pity, pride ("I am not getting what I want"), and a failure to acknowledge

PHYSICAL	SPIRITUAL
Insomnia or hypersomnia	Shame
Significant weight changes	Guilt
Feeling of being restless	Fear
or slowed down	Thanklessness
Fatigue, loss of energy	Unforgiving spirit
Problems concentrating	Hopelessness
Sense of alienation from things	Unbelief
once deemed beautiful and pleasant	Anger
Feeling sad, blue, down in the dumps	

Figure 7.2. Possible physical and spiritual symptoms in depression

God. In either case, thoughts of death or suicide can be addressed through God's Word.

A frequent feature of the cluster of depressive symptoms is anger. This does not appear in the technical definition of depression, but it is well documented in the literature on depression. Sometimes depression is related to being wronged by another person or not getting what you want. In these cases, a common response is anger toward the perpetrator and, ultimately, anger against God for giving hardships that "I don't deserve."

Address the Heart

Ministry to those who are depressed starts with compassion. When you listen closely to the experiences of those who are depressed, it sounds like a form of psychological torture. Even worse, since pain tends to isolate people, those who have symptoms of depression tend to feel very much alone, even alone from God. Given such a profile, the immediate response of God's Word is compassion. The church must move toward the depressed person and mourn with those who mourn (Rom. 12:15), pray for God's deliverance (2 Cor. 1:9–11), and search for encouraging words that can bless and give hope.

This response is obvious. It could be no other way. But the reason it must be highlighted with depression and other psychiatric complaints is that we are not naturally attracted to depressed people. If you have ever lived with a depressed person, you realize that friends and family begin to tire in their compassion and offers for help. For some friends and family, it is almost as if depression feels contagious—after a few weeks with a depressed person, *you* begin to feel depressed.

Be Alert to Spiritual Warfare

Compassion, of course, is much more than sympathizing with a person's pain. Compassion is active. It discerns. It knows the isolating nature of depression. To combat it, compassion considers ways to encourage faith and a knowledge of the presence of God. It knows that Satan is attracted to the inward-turning instincts of depression. It also knows that Satan wants to produce sullen atheists. Therefore, compassion must be ready to fight.

The question is, "How can we fix our eyes on Jesus in the midst of this suffering?" Or, to put it more practically, "How can we trust and obey in the midst of suffering?" Satan is going to be whispering that God does not hear, that he does not care, that he does not love. After all, what father would willingly let his child go through such an ordeal? In light of these whispers, the depressed person needs to know the exalted, loving God.

How can you help? How can you present Jesus in a way that is not condescending or oblivious to a person's pain? Consider simply asking depressed people how you can help them see Jesus. I have known depressed people who have had the following ideas:

➤ Be physically present.

➤ Pray with them.

➤ Clean the house with them.

➤ Read the Psalms together.

➤ Read some of the old hymns from a hymnbook.

➤ Go for a walk or exercise together.

Whichever ways you choose, always keep one eye open for the enemy who wants to use the same tactics he used in the book of Job. Satan persistently asks, "How can you trust and worship God when he has deprived you of earthly pleasure?"

Deal with Obvious Spiritual Problems

Compassion cannot ignore unbelief or sin. Too often, family and friends think the depressed person is very fragile and cannot handle any frank discussion about sin or hard-heartedness. But to ignore these issues when they are obvious in someone's life is to treat that person without love and compassion.

We often react negatively to this idea. Isn't this a case of beating people when they are down? Won't this crush their self-worth even more? If we find ourselves thinking this way, we are probably hearing the culture talking more than the Bible. The Bible always portrays our sin problem as being deeper than any pain we could experience. To ignore sin, especially when it is obvious, is to offer only a very superficial kind of love and compassion, and to withhold help that is needed at the deepest level.

Of course, the knowledge of sin must be accompanied by the knowledge of God's great, forgiving love. The psalmist says that his forgiveness is so amazing, so unlike our own, that it leaves us in awe and reverential fear (Ps. 130:4). When we grasp this forgiving love, we understand why Scripture considers repentance a path to liberation, not condemnation. It leads us to the light and away from the darkness. If the knowledge of sin crushes, it crushes our pride, not our selves.

Where might depressed people need spiritual teaching or rebuke? Hopeless people need to grow in a hope that looks past the temporal and on to the eternal. The ones who feel worthless may need to know that they are children of God by faith. They may also need to confess a pride that says, "I want more"—more money, more good looks, more relationships, more love, more respect. They might need to confess that these "I wants" have been for self-satisfaction and self-glory rather than the glory of God.

Feelings of guilt can also point to different underlying problems.

For example, some people simply need to know about the grace of God in Christ. They need to know that they stand before God because of the righteousness of Christ, not their own righteousness. They need to know that forgiveness of sins is not based on the quality of the confession, but on the quality of Christ's sacrifice. Too often, however, this encouraging teaching seems to leave the depressed person's guilt untouched.

There can be many reasons for this.

➤ The person may be involved in things for which he or she *should* feel guilty.

➤ The person does not believe what God says about forgiveness.

➤ The person wants to use guilt as a way to punish himself to pay back for his own sins. This betrays a heart of pride that thinks it can deal, in some small way, with its own sins.

Regardless of the reason, if guilt is part of the cluster of experiences that make up depression, it must be confronted. Guilt is an excellent warning light that says something is wrong. Yet when it persists too long, it provides fuel for Satan's lies and strangulates spiritual growth.

There are many other issues of the heart that will emerge during depression: anger, legalism, unbelief, lack of love for others, and so on. Some of these will be a result of the physical symptoms affecting the heart. That is, the physical symptoms test our hearts and expose them. This is different from saying that the physical symptoms *caused* these heart issues. They might *accompany* them rather than cause them. It is as if the pressure of difficult circumstances pushes the true condition of our heart to the surface. When the depressed person deals biblically with these issues, she is freed to grow in faith and obedience.

Will the depression be alleviated by dealing with these issues of the heart? We have no guarantees from Scripture. There is no promise that righteousness always leads to health. Although we can be confident that God gives grace to grow in faith, obedience, and even joy in the midst of suffering, we cannot have absolute confidence that the physical symptoms will disappear.

Sometimes, however, depression (both spiritual and *physical* symptoms) is caused by the heart. The spiritual-physical connection makes it clear that this is a possibility. If so, as the depressed person understands spiritual truth, turns away from sin, and follows Christ in faith, then the experience of depression will gradually fade.

Medical Treatments for Depression

If depression consisted solely of spiritual problems, there would be no reason to talk about medication and other physical treatments. But depression *does* have physical symptoms. Therefore, medical treatments might be helpful to ease or erase the physical symptoms of depression (and those of other psychiatric problems). In this generation, there are a handful of treatments available. None of them helps all the time. All of them can have harmful side effects.

The best known medical treatments are the antidepressant drugs. This group includes well-known drugs such as Prozac, Elavil, and Desyrel. There is no evidence that these drugs treat a specific chemical deficiency that causes depression in people, but there is evidence that these drugs can change some depressive *symptoms* in some people.

There are dozens of other treatments available that might help in some cases. Diet, megavitamins, full spectrum lights, and shock treatments are among the more common. Each has been helpful for some people, but each has its opponents. If you struggle with depression, you are often willing to try just about anything for some relief. Before you do, make sure you get plenty of information about the treatment.

I would suggest the following guidelines for counselors when considering physical treatments:

1. If the person is already taking medication, don't do anything unless he or she is having harmful or uncomfortable side effects. Remember that it is neither sinful nor a sign of spiritual weakness to take medication.

If the depressed person has had more trouble *after* taking the medication, then suggest that he consult with the prescribing physician. If he seems to have benefited from the medication, or if the medication is doing nothing, then you as the helper or friend can focus on more important issues. Focus on spiritual encouragement, growth in faith and obedience, and hope. Depression, like any form of suffering, is always a time when we should expect God to teach us.

If the depressed person grows in faith and obedience, then you might want to suggest that she consult with her physician about her medication. If the medication is not helping, there is no reason to take it. If the medication helped initially, it is possible that it is no longer useful. Or there may have been spiritual roots to the depression that have been addressed. When consulted on this, some physicians might reply that it is best to continue the medication. Others suggest a plan to go off it gradually. If the depressive symptoms forcefully emerge during this process, the person can simply go back to the previous level of medication and try to stop at a later time.

2. If the person is not taking medication but is considering it, I typically suggest that he or she postpone that decision for a period of time. During that time, I consider possible causes, and together we ask God to teach us about both ourselves and him so that we can grow in faith in the midst of hardship. If the depression persists, I might let the person know that medication is an option to deal with some of the physical symptoms.

3. If the person is growing spiritually but is still depressed, and if medication is not helping, I suggest that he or she consider other possible problems. Scores of medical problems can lead to depression:

Parkinson's disease, multiple sclerosis, lupus, hepatitis, electrolyte abnormalities from anorexia, and others. The most frequent physical cause of depression is the side effects of prescription medication. Blood pressure and heart medication, antibacterial drugs, and psychiatric drugs are common culprits.

The clues that suggest a possible physical cause for depression are as follows:

➤ The person is over age forty.

➤ There is no history of previous problems with depression.

➤ The person's circumstances are largely unchanged.

➤ The person is taking prescription drugs.

If someone meets these criteria, then suggest a medical consultation.

A Case Study

Susan's depression was literally killing her. For years it just seemed to get worse and worse. Now, this single, thirty-two-year-old woman was down to ninety-eight pounds and could barely drag herself to the school where she taught special education. What was remarkable about her depression was that no one knew. Susan preferred to put on a happy exterior when she was at work, at church, or with friends. It was only when a friend started asking about her health and probing as to how she was doing that someone finally "got in" to Susan's life.

What Susan's friend found was an unceasing, painful depression that was immune to all medication. (Susan had tried.) For weeks, they prayed for relief. They also prayed that God would teach both of them through the depression, whether it persisted or not. Admittedly, this was a hard prayer for Susan, but both women believed it was how the Bible taught them to pray.

Such a prayer leads to answers. Susan had had an abortion ten years before, right around the time she was becoming a Christian. She knew it was wrong, but she felt as if she had no choice. With the encouragement of a few friends, she terminated the pregnancy.

Many women have abortions and don't get depressed. Some just try to forget about it and move on; others eventually know forgiveness. Susan could do neither. Her depression began after the abortion and it had been gathering momentum ever since. She couldn't forget, and she didn't believe that she could be completely forgiven.

The answer seemed obvious: Susan needed to know that God forgives sins. She had already confessed this as part of what she believed as a Christian. In fact, she had confessed it at least weekly for the previous ten years. Now it was time to learn specifically about the riches of God's grace.

The two women began to talk and read Scripture about the forgiveness of sins. They would meet weekly, pray for each other, and commit themselves to growing in this great truth. For Susan's friend, it was great. She was growing in joy as she realized that she had been forgiven for much. Susan, however, seemed unaffected. After a few months, Susan's friend said something only a friend can say.

"Susan, sometimes it seems like depression is your friend. You don't want to let it go. It almost seems like you get something from it."

Susan was curious rather than angry. "What do you mean?"

"I mean, here we have been talking about things that seem to go to the heart of your depression, but they don't bring life to you. You respond as if these truths are good for me but not for you. You are a great counselor to me, but you don't apply them to yourself.

"Why don't you want to believe these things? Do you think your sin is beyond God's forgiveness?"

"Yes, I have often thought that."

"Susan, I wonder if your depression is your way of trying to say that you are sorry."

"Yes, I think it is. Isn't that okay?"

"Well, it sounds okay, but doesn't it really mean that you think you can meet God halfway? God pays for the little sins but you help him with the big ones. If that is what's happening, then the root is your own pride—thinking that you can somehow do penance for your sins."

Susan smiled a genuine smile for the first time in years. Her friend's comments were right on target. She felt as if God had graciously exposed her. The problem was that she needed to *confess her righteousness*. She thought that there was some spiritual capital or righteousness within her that she could use to pay God back for her sin. Spiritual growth, however, begins when we say that we have nothing with which to repay our spiritual debt.

Susan's depression lifted almost immediately. Seven years later she remains free from the pain that held her for over a decade. In her case, the physical symptoms of depression had a spiritual cause.

Of course, not all depression has a spiritual cause. My own observation is that a large percentage of it does, but don't let that cause you to think that all depression is caused by spiritual problems. When you confront depression, all you know is that it is painful, and any time people suffer, they are likely to encounter a more obvious spiritual battle. You also know that suffering is a time when we can ask God to search us and help us grow in faith. Sometimes during that search, spiritual problems will emerge that actually have caused the depression. At other times, spiritual problems will emerge that coincide with but are not caused by the depression. And still other times you will find great faith and obedience coexisting with depression, in which case you continue to encourage the person in faith and hope.

CHAPTER 8

ATTENTION DEFICIT DISORDER

CONCERNED and puzzled parents have made attention deficit/ hyperactivity disorder (ADD or ADHD) the best known psychiatric diagnosis ever. Books on the topic in public libraries seldom return to the shelves. Waiting lists keep them almost perpetually checked out. In an effort to better understand and help their children, parents have turned to seminars, news reports, and TV shows for information. Computer networks have bulletin boards devoted to the topic. To add to this interest, many adults are finding that ADD applies to them, too. Adults who are intellectually capable but "never measured up to their potential" have found in ADD a category that makes all the seemingly disparate pieces of their lives finally fit together. Rarely does any literature leave so many readers thinking, "So *that's* been the problem!"

As with everything we read and hear, Christians should assimilate this information with biblical discernment. The material on ADD is often interesting and helpful, but it is not Scripture. Therefore, it can be prone to unbiblical assumptions and errors. For example, some books on ADD abolish the words "bad" or "sinful." Other books use a biological approach, claiming that brain functioning explains every behavior. What follows is an overview and some biblical guidelines

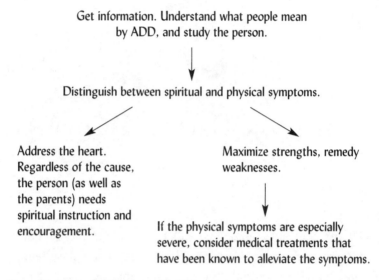

Get information. Understand what people mean
by ADD, and study the person.

Distinguish between spiritual and physical symptoms.

Address the heart. Regardless of the cause, the person (as well as the parents) needs spiritual instruction and encouragement.

Maximize strengths, remedy weaknesses.

If the physical symptoms are especially severe, consider medical treatments that have been known to alleviate the symptoms.

Figure 8.1. Steps to helping those with ADD symptoms

that can help you understand the symptoms that have recently been called ADD.

The strategy is the same as that for depression (Figure 8.1).

What Is ADD?

The technical definition of ADD has evolved over the last few decades. Its present form highlights three main symptoms: inattention, hyperactivity, and impulsivity.[1] To receive the label, you must demonstrate inattention, hyperactivity-impulsivity, or both.

---

1 The APA definition can be found in *Diagnostic Criteria from DSM-IV* (Washington, D.C.: American Psychiatric Association, 1994). This definition is more lenient than that of the World Health Organization (WHO). The WHO, which uses the ICD-10 classification system, labels many of the American cases as "conduct disorder."

A. Either (1) or (2):

(1) Six (or more) of the following symptoms of inattention have persisted for at least six months to a degree that is maladaptive and inconsistent with developmental level:

Inattention
   (a) Often makes careless mistakes in schoolwork, work, or other activities.
   (b) Often has difficulty sustaining attention in tasks or play activities.
   (c) Often does not seem to listen when spoken to directly.
   (d) Often does not follow through on instructions and fails to finish schoolwork, chores, or duties in the workplace (not due to oppositional behavior or failure to understand instructions).
   (e) Often has difficulty organizing tasks and activities.
   (f) Often avoids, dislikes, or is reluctant to engage in tasks that require sustained mental effort (such as schoolwork or homework).
   (g) Often loses things necessary for tasks or activities (e.g., toys, school assignments, pencils, books, or tools).
   (h) Is often easily distracted by extraneous stimuli.
   (i) Is often forgetful in daily activities.

(2) Six (or more) of the following symptoms of hyperactivity-impulsivity have persisted for at least six months to a degree that is maladaptive and inconsistent with developmental level:

Hyperactivity
   (a) Often fidgets with hands or feet or squirms in seat.
   (b) Often leaves seat in classroom or in other situations in which remaining seated is expected.

(c) Often runs about or climbs excessively in situations in which it is inappropriate (in adolescents or adults, may be limited to subjective feelings of restlessness).

(d) Often has difficulty playing or engaging in leisure activities quietly.

(e) Is often "on the go" or often acts as if "driven by a motor."

(f) Often talks excessively.

Impulsivity

(g) Often blurts out answers before questions have been completed.

(h) Often has difficulty awaiting turn.

(i) Often interrupts or intrudes on others (e.g., butts into conversations or games).

B. Some hyperactive-impulsive or inattentive symptoms that caused impairment were present before age seven years.

C. Some impairment from the symptoms is present in two or more settings (e.g., at school [or work] and at home).

D. There must be clear evidence of clinically significant impairment in social, academic, or occupational functioning.[2]

Have you just read your autobiography? It seems to fit your typical driven American. The word "often" allows many of us to sneak into the category. Researchers, however, prefer to reserve the term for more extreme behaviors.

For example, children (and adults) seem to have mouths (and arms, hands, and legs!) that run ahead of their thinking. (Or, their

2 *Diagnostic Criteria from DSM-IV,* 63–64.

thinking is distracted and darts from one place to another. Their body is just trying to keep up.) As a friend of mine said, "He doesn't sleep, he recharges." Caring for young boys who fit these descriptions makes you feel as if you are spinning a dozen plates in the air. Parents often manage the problem by withdrawing their children from situations where they will embarrass them or be too rough with other children. Do you want them to sit politely at the table while the adults leisurely eat their meal and discuss the day? Forget it. It will be painful for everybody.

With younger girls, ADD symptoms are less noticeable because, while they may be highly distractible, they are less likely to be hyperactive. As a result, they stare out the school windows, don't disturb their classmates, and go unnoticed for years.

Older children can be maddening in that they can be fixated on the television or Nintendo for hours, but they can concentrate on their homework for ten seconds or less. In other words, their attention is *inconsistent* rather than universally poor. It is as if their attention needs props such as a fast pace, excitement, and constant feedback. For these children, boredom is death. They might provoke Mom or engage in some physically dangerous activity just to make life more interesting.

At school, they seem constantly disorganized. Their assignments are hastily done. They lose their lunch money or their house keys. Their patient teachers may love them and always talk about how much potential they have, but the same teachers may feel as if they are going crazy at times.

Adults with these symptoms have lives that are often characterized by chronic difficulties meeting deadlines, frequent job changes (they are either bored or fired), impulsive decisions, inaccurate insights into personal strengths and weaknesses, and inaccurate insights into the ways others respond to them. They talk as if everything is going great, they talk about new plans, but they tend to be filled with self-doubt.

With these descriptions, it is easy to understand why there is so much interest in ADD. Parents as well as adults who loosely fit the profile are looking for anything that will help.

Distinguish Between Physical and Spiritual

If someone suggests that your child (or you) displays behaviors consistent with ADD, don't panic. Translate ADD as, "It is time to develop a deeper understanding of this person." Don't let the label cause you to think that you now understand the labeled person. You are just *beginning* to study him.

Both the spiritual and the physical must be taken seriously. If you ignore the spiritual, there will never be a place for repentance and faith in your child's life. Sinful behavior will be excused. The power of the Gospel will be ignored. If you ignore physical or brain-based strengths and weaknesses, you will never find the creative methods you need to help the person learn. When the teaching style is poorly suited to the individual, he or she will soon be confused and hopeless.

Like all children, those labeled ADD have strengths and weaknesses. Strengths (talents, abilities) might include

➤ a high energy level,

➤ an infectious enthusiasm for certain tasks,

➤ unusual creativity and ability to generate ideas,

➤ a willingness to take risks,

➤ an outgoing personality.

Weaknesses sometimes apparent in ADD-labeled children include

➤ poor memory for the spoken or written word,

➤ difficulty sequencing behavior or devising steps to complete a task,

> difficulty establishing priorities,

> difficulty with sustained attention when tasks are not intrinsically interesting,

> difficulty screening out irrelevant stimuli,

> difficulty changing from one way of thinking to another (mental flexibility),

> poor insight into these weaknesses and strengths.

With many children labeled ADD, the arena of the heart is ignored. Yet isn't it possible that some of what we call ADD is sinful self-indulgence and laziness? Is it possible that a prominent cause of the behaviors is a heart that demands its own way? The truth is that ADD sits at an intersection where physical and spiritual meet. Like other psychiatric labels, the root cause may be physical *or* spiritual; it is typically both.

Does it sound harsh to suggest that sin may be a cause of what is popularly called ADD? Might such an explanation damage children, as some secular investigators suggest? I think not. If sin is called sin, this can bring hope for change. Furthermore, most children have a conscience that is alert to right and wrong. To say that something is wrong is to tell them something they already know. What *can* be hurtful and confusing is when something is called sinful or wrong, but it should more accurately be called a limitation or a weakness.

Keep asking the question, "Am I certain that this behavior transgresses God's law?" If so, then the behavior is rooted in a spiritual problem. Say, for example, that your child is hitting another child because the other child is playing with his toy. This is clearly a spiritual problem. Your child might *also* struggle with inattention and hyperactivity-impulsivity, but these cannot be excuses for such behavior. Physical problems do not force a child to sin.

Chapter Eight

Conscience Versus Comprehension

What if a child is jumping all over the tables in the school cafeteria when there is a school rule that you don't stand on the tables? In this situation, the child is disobeying the cafeteria monitor. Is that all we need to know? What if the child has a room in his house where he is allowed to jump all over the furniture? Would that make any difference? Don't forget that mental flexibility is a complex brain process. It is possible that he has forgotten the rule and is operating on his knowledge of the rules from home.

In this case, it would be wise to speak with the child before he goes to the cafeteria, remind him of the rule, and perhaps have the cafeteria monitor close by for a few days. This way, the monitor can touch the child or speak his name—any cue that will help the boy remember to practice self-control in the cafeteria.

Although the physical and spiritual categories are distinct, you can see that discerning the way each of them contributes to troublesome behavior can be challenging. Let's say, for example, that you told your child to clean his room. When you return twenty minutes later, he is still playing with toys amid the chaos. Is this a spiritual problem? On the surface, it would certainly seem so. The child has violated the command to obey his parents. Yet there might be other explanations. Perhaps the child does not know how to "clean his room"—the idea might be too general and abstract. Perhaps his room looks perfectly clean to him, or perhaps he started to clean the room and then was distracted by a favorite toy. In other words, what you may be seeing is a weakness in the child's ability to follow through with the directions rather than overt disobedience.

There is a difference between telling a child, "Clean your room" and "Don't hit your brother." The child has a conscience and intuitively knows that he should not hit others in anger. Such an act would be wrong even if a parent did not say, "Don't hit." But the child does not have a conscience that says it is morally wrong to leave an unkempt room. The unkempt room is technically a violation of the command to obey one's parents, but in some cases, disobedience is not the relevant biblical category. An understanding of the child's heart might indicate that the problem is physical limitations (e.g., memory problems) and ignorance, not spiritual rebellion. There are never excuses for sinful anger and unloving behavior, but sometimes there *are* excuses for not cleaning your room.

What if a child is disruptive at the dinner table? It may be that the child is naturally more active but is *also* unwilling to listen to parental instruction. In such cases, parents must know how to address both a sinful heart *and* an energetic constitution. All of a sudden, parenting is becoming complicated.

But a biblical perspective simplifies. Biblical parenting is time-consuming, and it relies on counsel from others, but it is not necessarily complicated. With the distinction between physical and spiritual problems in mind, take steps to grow in nurturing your child in the Lord. No matter what your child's strengths and weaknesses, he has the same spiritual problem as everyone else: his heart is in a war between selfishness and obedience to Christ. Like yourself, a child engages this battle with (1) the knowledge of Christ and (2) obedience to Christ. The knowledge of Christ consists of learning about the great justice and love of God displayed in Jesus' death and resurrection. Obedience to Christ is our response to this good news. It consists of practicing the command to love God and love your neighbor as yourself, two commands that are fleshed out by the Ten Commandments and other clear principles in Scripture.

Establishing Priorities

For children who tend to be more impulsive in their speech or actions, some biblical principles might deserve special emphasis. The parental task is to develop priorities among the various biblical principles and stay focused on the ones that are most important for the child's spiritual needs. It is wiser to take one principle and work with it intensively for a few months than it is to work with ten principles superficially, leaving them undeveloped, unclear, and not regularly prayed for.

James 1:19 is at the top of many parental lists. It is uniquely suited to those who tend to be more distractible and impulsive: "Everyone should be quick to listen, slow to speak, and slow to become angry." This triad may take years to master, but if God requires such behaviors, he will give grace to accomplish them.

As these children move into their teen and adult years, other principles might become more important. Since some children have minds that tend to fly from one thing to another or prefer the spontaneous to the planned and orderly, it might be especially important for them to learn the biblical principle of perseverance.

Other teens and adults might be horrible at prioritizing work. They might consistently overestimate their ability to do a particular task. These individuals must learn the biblical principle of being teachable and seeking the counsel of others: "Plans fail for lack of counsel, but with many advisers they succeed" (Prov. 15:22).

As you gain proficiency in spiritual nurture and discipleship, turn your attention to the person's unique strengths and weaknesses. Start by getting as much information on your child as possible. Don't be embarrassed: talk with school teachers, Sunday school teachers, baby sitters, and friends. Ask the school for educational testing. The more you understand about the particular strengths and weaknesses of the person, the better you can creatively teach and apply relevant biblical principles. For example, if your child does better with pictures and concrete, visual explanations than he does with oral instructions, you might role-play how to be kind to a younger sibling rather than simply telling him that he should "be kind." "Hear it, see it, do it" is the parent's or educator's rule of thumb.

The Need for Structure

Many of the practical suggestions for dealing with those who are distractible or who tend to bounce from one activity to another can be summarized with the word *structure*. Structure refers to boundaries, guidelines, reminders, and limits. It is a fence that can help contain and direct. Since some children have a style of thinking that is chaotic, disorganized, and unreliable, structure compensates by providing external controls. Without structure, the constant change and ambiguous expectations magnify every small difficulty.

Structure means having predictable, clear, simple, and written household rules. These rules should be rehearsed weekly with the child and consistently enforced. Avoid lengthy, abstract explanations. If you tend to deliver monologues, don't. If you need time to develop a particular teaching or explain a form of discipline, dialogue with the child to keep his attention. Ask him questions. Have him read Scripture out loud. Ask him to explain where he disobeyed. When giving instructions, make sure the child is paying attention; have him look you in the eyes, then ask him to repeat the instructions. You might even review his plan for carrying out the instructions.

Structure means that instead of constantly reacting to problems (which can increase the sense of chaos), you pre-empt them. Although the child may have difficulty anticipating future problems, you should be alert to the places where he habitually stumbles. You know from experience where there will be difficulties. If the difficult situation cannot or should not be avoided, prepare the child to face it with prayer and practice. Then, after the difficult time is over (e.g., homework, chores), give the child feedback so that he can see his progress.

These guidelines are relevant to adults as well. For the adult who tends to have difficulty sustaining attention or devising plans, structure means establishing routines, such as doing three difficult but necessary tasks before more enjoyable jobs. It means setting reasonable deadlines (under the guidance of others) and meeting them. Well-prioritized "to do" lists are a must.

Medical Treatments

If you have diligently pursued these suggestions but are still troubled by the severity of a child's hyperactivity or distractibility (especially if those behaviors are dramatically affecting school performance), then you might consult with a knowledgeable physician. There *are* some medical problems that can provoke ADD symptoms. For example, thyroid problems can affect energy level, and hearing or visual impairments can make paying attention difficult. A good physical exam can rule these out.

The vast majority of ADD-labeled children will have normal physical exams, but many physicians will suggest a medical treatment anyway. The treatment is typically stimulant drugs such as Ritalin or antidepressants such as Norpramin (Desipramine) or Prozac.

That a stimulant drug would help some children focus seems paradoxical. You would expect that children would be even more physically and mentally excitable when taking it. However, at the commonly prescribed doses, everyone tends to have better performances on certain simple mental tasks, and children in particular seem to be less fidgety.

How does Ritalin do this? We know that Ritalin affects a number of areas in the brain, but its mode of action is uncertain. One thing, however, is clear. Ritalin *does not* treat any known chemical deficiency in a child's brain. No one needs Ritalin. Like most psychiatric drugs (including the antidepressants discussed earlier), the best analogy would be to say that Ritalin-type drugs act like aspirin: they suppress symptoms in some people, but they are not a cure.

Most experts agree that Ritalin-type drugs are overprescribed. They argue that ADD itself is overdiagnosed; they see that our culture is quick to treat any behavior with drugs, and they fear that physicians are quick to dispense such a relatively safe drug to children whose parents are looking for a quick fix. This does not mean that we must avoid the drug. It does mean, however, that as the American Pediatric Association suggests, we consider it *after* examining other factors in the child's life.

Should Christian parents consider this medication for their children? If you consult a cross-section of the Christian population you will hear "definitely yes," "definitely no, under any circumstances," and everything in between. Such differences of opinion among committed, thinking Christians suggest, at least, that Scripture does not clearly say no. The question is more "Is it wise?" than "Is it wrong?"

In order to make a wise choice, there is information to consider. Ritalin is one of the safer prescription drugs. It was first used with hyperactive children in the 1930s, and so it has a long history. It is now prescribed to over two million people, and we are familiar with its side effects.

The most common side effects of Ritalin are the suppression of appetite and loss of sleep. Since these side effects are dose-related, they can sometimes be avoided by lowering the dose. Another troubling (though rare) side effect is involuntary muscle twitching. These twitches too might disappear with a lower dose. If not, they will disappear when the medication is discontinued.

At its best, Ritalin can help an individual focus better, sustain efforts over a longer period of time, moderate mood swings, and reduce distractibility. At its worst, it has side effects without beneficial effects.

It was once assumed that Ritalin improved school performance, but the evidence does not yet clearly support this assumption. Although Ritalin is praised by many elementary school teachers, and some children demonstrate significant behavioral changes, there is little evidence that Ritalin significantly improves academic performance. After two years of taking Ritalin, many children who receive the drug perform at about the same level as their ADD-labeled counterparts who do not.

It is imperative to stress that drugs cannot change a child's heart. If a child seems more obedient when taking Ritalin, it is because an influence on the child's life has changed. That is, in the same way that parents and peers can influence our hearts, so our bodies can influence us. Our bodies bring pleasure and pain, intellectual clarity and confusion. Such physical changes can act like a temptation to which some children respond sinfully. When the temptation is removed, these children might be less prone to certain kinds of sins.

If you do choose to try Ritalin-type drugs, the most important principle is that your quest for medical treatment must not outdistance your diligence in spiritual nurture. No matter how profound the physical weaknesses may be, they cannot keep your child from growing in obedience and the knowledge of Christ. That fact should offer hope and encouragement in your discipling of your child, as well as limit your expectations about what medication will do for him.

Some parents seek alternative medical treatments such as diet or megavitamins. Wisdom is again the rule. If you pursue these treatments, don't let them substitute for spiritual nurture, and be careful how much time and money you invest. They are helpful only in very select cases.

Parenting those with ADD symptoms is ultimately like parenting any child: you accommodate your biblical instruction to the child's abilities. Parenting children who are like us is relatively straightforward because we instinctively understand their strengths and weaknesses. But children whose strengths and weaknesses are out of the mainstream require more careful observation and creative teaching. Remember that these children too have God-given strengths, and whatever weaknesses they have will not slow their growth in the things that are most important.

A Case Study

A few years ago my family visited a family in our church. The husband had been taking illegal drugs—amphetamines in particular—and had recently confessed his drug use, gone through detoxification, and said he was committed to staying away from drugs. After years of neglect, his family was in chaos.

As we went into the house, the first thing we noticed was that the interior had been gutted. There were projects, half-completed, going on throughout the entire house. When we mentioned that they were busy with home construction, the wife nonchalantly (or in tired resignation) said that it had been going on for years! She appeared to be accustomed to the disarray. Apparently, her husband would have grand ideas to completely remake the house, but then would quickly get bored with the project. Occasionally, when they expected company or when his wife became angry, he would work through the night and make progress on a few of the projects, but he never persisted. It was as if he would get bored and want to move on to something else.

Can you see a pattern emerging? This man looked and talked as if he were still taking amphetamines, which he was not. He wouldn't sit for more than a minute at a time. He was a flurry of movement, darting from playing with the children, then back to our conversation. I was actually getting tired as I was sitting there. He could have been a poster boy for the symptoms of ADD. It made you wonder if amphetamines were his drug of choice because he felt that it gave his world a little *more* order.

Where do you begin? My friend first had to realize that there was a problem, and he quickly acknowledged this. Maybe too quickly. But we set off on a course of action. I kept thinking "structure," both physical and spiritual. Structure around his scattered style of thought and structure around his heart: "Above all else, guard your heart, for it is the wellspring of life" (Prov. 4:23).

For his heart, he began daily times of Bible reading and prayer. In order to keep on task, he wrote down one thing he learned from his reading and parts of his prayers. He found that if he didn't write down a structure for his prayers, he would mentally drift to other topics. In order to provide feedback and further structure, I reviewed his weekly journals. He started his study in the book of Proverbs.

There was a small group of families from the church that met near his house on Tuesday evenings. He decided, along with his wife, that such a midweek meeting would be essential.

Next we turned our attention to his brain weaknesses. We decided that the house was the place to start. We asked what projects his wife most wanted to see completed. Then we enlisted the help of a contractor at the church who mapped out which projects should be done first, how much time each project would take, and whether professional help was needed. On the basis of his suggestions, we established a series of "to do" steps. My friend was to work on the house for ten hours a week, and he would contract out the work that he did not want to do. After the first week we realized that we needed to specify exactly when those ten hours would be and to set specific goals for each unit of work.

Looking back, God was very gracious in teaching both of us. We have both changed through the years together. To summarize some of what we have learned, and where we have failed, three things come to mind. First, we both realize how critical it is to maintain the fear of the Lord as our heart's motivation. This is not being afraid of God; rather, it is a reverential awe and obedience that comes from the knowledge of his great justice and love. Second, we realize that spiritual growth demands constant attention. Too often, we would have spurts where we would get together frequently and then let a few weeks slip by without any accountability. Third, we realize that when we established goals for marriage, family, home projects, or church service, we needed to be very specific and develop specific steps to attain them.

Applying These Steps to Other Psychiatric Problems

With this basic approach, you have a way to deal with most psychiatric problems. You even have a way to minister to problems as bizarre as schizophrenia. Following the steps already outlined, you begin like this:

1. Understand the experience of schizophrenia.
2. Distinguish between physical and spiritual issues. Physical symptoms include hallucinations, delusions, altered sensory experience, and problems synthesizing information. Spiritual symptoms include sinful response to hallucinations, lack of concern for others, and guilt.
3. Deal biblically with the obvious spiritual problems. The least that is possible is that the person can grow in faith and obedience in the midst of the other symptoms. It is also possible that spiritual problems have caused the physical symptoms, in which case spiritual change may reduce those symptoms.
4. Encourage and show compassion as the person wrestles with the more physical symptoms. If they persist, consider medical treatment.

Schizophrenia, ADD, depression, premenstrual syndrome (PMS), manic episodes, borderline personality, and other symptoms have been named and claimed by psychiatry but are in fact overseen by Scripture. When theological categories are clarified and applied, Scripture does an amazing job at illuminating existing research. But it does more. Scripture alone goes all the way to the heart.

The Brain Didn't *Do It:*
New Trends in the Brain Sciences

CHAPTER

HOMOSEXUALITY[1]

"THE evidence for a 'gay' gene is increasing."[2] So proclaims an international magazine after reporting that the second wave of studies—those trying to replicate earlier landmark ones—are beginning to give possible support to the gay gene theory.

If a gene were found for Alzheimer's disease, we would not be surprised. Memory impairment, speech problems, lack of coordination, and disorientation are physical problems, and so we would not be surprised to find physical causes for them. If a gene were found for depression or ADD, we *might* be surprised. Despite the physical symptoms associated with these labels, there are so many types of depression and ADD that we would not expect to blame them all on genetics. And we've seen that both depression and ADD have spiritual components and possibly spiritual causes.

But what about homosexuality? Is the evidence increasing for a

---

1 Homosexuality can be defined as thoughts or actions, in adult life, motivated by a definite erotic (sexual-genital-orgiastic) attraction to members of the same sex, usually but not necessarily leading to sexual relations with them. Even though there are differences between male and female homosexuality, I will use the term "homosexual" to refer to male or female unless otherwise indicated.

2 "Thanks, Mum," *The Economist,* 4 November 1995, 87.

causative gene? In ten to fifteen years will everyone just assume that homosexuality is based on brain differences?

Homosexuality is *the* hot issue in the church and society. Even more than abortion, it will confront the church throughout this generation. Political sanctions will be imposed on institutions that refuse to hire homosexuals. Homosexuals will probably have their "place at the table" with civil recognition of same-sex marriages.[3] Under the heading of "pluralism," all forms of sexual expression will be considered equally valid. Church leaders will continue to be "outed." More denominations will revise their exegesis of biblical passages to allow for homosexual relationships.[4] And people who otherwise take the Bible seriously will leave churches that call homosexuality "sin." Certainly, throughout its history the church has faced persecution and criticism from the world, but at no time has the church so routinely been denounced as "evil" for upholding what appear to be biblical principles. Clearly, the nature of the topic demands humility and careful thought.

The approach to homosexuality that follows will include principles similar to those already established. First, understand the person. Second, distinguish between spiritual and physical symptoms. Third, address the heart issues. Fourth, if it is relevant, address the physical problems (Figure 9.1).

What Does the Bible Say About Homosexuality?

On this topic in particular, we must start with the question, "What does God say?" Since the debate is as much over the interpretation of Scripture as it is the scientific studies, this is where we must be will-

---

3 Bruce Bawer, *A Place at the Table: The Gay Individual in American Society* (New York: Poseidon, 1994).
4 The statements on homosexuality of more than forty-five different denominations can be found in J. Gordon Melton, *The Church Speaks Out on: Homosexuality* (Detroit: Gale Research, 1991).

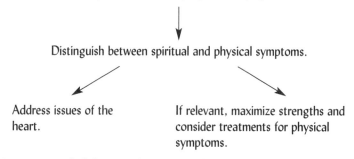

Figure 9.1. Steps for helping people regardless of their problem

ing to dialogue. Is it possible that the church has been led by an anti-homosexual culture rather than clear biblical principles? It is possible, since sinners can certainly err in their interpretation of Scripture. So our discussion will begin with a re-examination of biblical passages.

At the outset, however, we must be clear that although the church *can* err in its interpretation of the Bible and is happy to be corrected, it stands under the Word of God. We must not give away any ground regarding the authority of Scripture. Admittedly, God's Word is not always easy to apply, but with the Holy Spirit as the interpreter, we should expect to reach unity among those who truly want to know what God says about this important subject. The goal is discovering "Thus says the Lord."[5] Our presuppositions are rooted not in emotivism but in the teaching of Scripture.

Even with the different grids through which we see, it is fairly easy to agree with homosexuals on one point: the Bible is unambiguous

---

5 Oxford University professor Alister McGrath indicates rightly that we live in a time when "openness and relevance are more important than truth. This, however, is intellectual shallowness and moral irresponsibility." Michael Foucault has similarly observed that "truth" in a post-modern world is nothing more than a compliment.

and consistent in its prohibitions against homosexuality. At every mention, it is condemned as sin.

Do not lie with a man as one lies with a woman; that is detestable. (Lev. 18:22)

If a man lies with a man as one lies with a woman, both of them have done what is detestable. They must be put to death; their blood will be on their own heads. (Lev. 20:13)

Because of this [idolatry], God gave them over to shameful lusts. Even their women exchanged natural relations for unnatural ones. In the same way the men also abandoned natural relations with women and were inflamed with lust for one another. (Rom. 1:26–27)

Do not be deceived: Neither the sexually immoral nor idolaters nor adulterers nor male prostitutes nor homosexual offenders [arsenokoitai]⁶ . . . will inherit the kingdom of God. (1 Cor. 6: 9–10)

. . . Law is made not for good men but for lawbreakers and rebels, the ungodly and sinful, . . . for adulterers and perverts [arsenokoitai]. . . . (1 Tim. 1:9)

. . . Sodom and Gomorrah and the surrounding towns gave themselves up to sexual immorality and perversion. They serve as an example of those who suffer the punishment of eternal fire. (Jude 7)

---

6 Some suggest that the meaning of *arsenokoitai* is unclear. However, Robin Scroggs, in *The New Testament and Homosexuality* (Philadelphia: Fortress Press), 106–8, has shown that the word is derived directly from Leviticus 18:22 and 20:13 and is used in rabbinic texts to refer to homosexual intercourse.

Some students of Scripture believe that a prohibition against homosexuality in Jesus' own words would make the case more conclusive. Jesus did not speak against homosexuality specifically, but neither did he specifically address many other sexual behaviors, such as incest, bestiality, and rape. That doesn't mean that they were permissible. Jesus consistently upheld the Old Testament law. He stood against all legalistic attempts to narrow its intent, and he maintained that the law addressed both behavior and attitude. He consistently spoke for marriage, and he indicated that the only alternative to heterosexual marriage was celibacy (Matt. 19:12).

Furthermore, Jesus' ministry demonstrated that he was an advocate of oppressed groups such as the poor, the physically afflicted, and women. Had he approved of homosexual relationships, his failure to say so would be a blatant omission in an otherwise "progressive" ministry that was never swayed by the criticisms of other people or larger cultural sins.

Yet the response of most homosexuals to these passages tends to be, "What does this have to do with me?" It is as if you are speaking to a group of twentieth-century pastors about how to distinguish between clean and unclean animals. The passages are considered irrelevant. That is because the homosexual hermeneutic—the pro-homosexual way to interpret Scripture—sees these verses as speaking only against "unnatural," noncommitted sexual relationships. The prohibitions allegedly do not apply to committed, loving relationships.

The reasoning goes like this: The Bible does not speak about "natural" homosexuality. It addresses only "unnatural" cultic male prostitution or "unnatural" homosexuality practiced by heterosexually oriented people.[7] The Bible does not speak specifically to people who are

---

7 For example, J. Nelson, "Homosexuality and the Church: Towards a Sexual Ethic of Love," *Christianity and Crisis* 37 (1977): 63–69.

oriented toward homosexuality. Therefore, in order to develop a biblical theology of homosexuality, other, more relevant Scripture must be examined. These relevant texts, it is argued, can be found in teaching about heterosexual relationships.

The biblical principle is that sexual behavior is the privilege of committed, loving relationships. For heterosexuals, sexual relationships occur only in the context of marriage. For homosexuals, lacking the legal sanction of marriage, sexual relationships should occur only (they say) when there is some kind of love for or loyalty to the same-sex partner. Casual homosexual or heterosexual relationships are wrong, but sex within marriage or a marriage-like relationship is good.

There are variations on this logic. For example, some suggest that homosexuality is prohibited in the Old and New Testament cultures, but the guidelines are no longer in force today because they were applicable mainly to a time when procreation was essential. Whatever the variation, the homosexual hermeneutic always makes two assumptions: (1) There is a "natural" homosexual orientation that is not addressed in Scripture, and (2) the biblical prohibitions against homosexuality are not applicable to modern homosexual "marriages."

This hermeneutic may seem absurd to many Christians. It sounds like the logic of a drinker who says that all the biblical references to drunkenness are irrelevant to him because he is an alcoholic (more on that in the next chapter). But the logic must not be discarded too quickly if we are going to answer the questions that led homosexuals to these conclusions. Doesn't it seem that many homosexuals have no choice in the matter? Aren't they born with that orientation? And isn't it true that there are differences between biblical times and now? Don't we consider some biblical passages to be time-limited cultural applications of truth rather than eternal moral verities? For example, many churches do not require women to wear head coverings or be silent despite 1 Corinthians 11. Why? Because they believe that the

Corinthian church was part of a unique culture with distinct ways of expressing submission. The eternal principle is submission, not coverings. But if we can do that with coverings, why not with homosexuality?

Was Biblical Homosexuality "Unnatural" and Is Modern-Day Homosexuality "Natural"?

Current arguments rely heavily on the idea that modern homosexuality is "natural." It is a God-given orientation, not unlike left-handedness. Homosexuality is not something that moderns *do,* it is who they *are.* The "shameful lusts" mentioned in Romans 1:26 refer (they say) to reckless *homo*sexual behavior by people oriented *hetero*sexually. This argument is essential to the homosexual position: homosexuality is an identity. Nobody chooses it. It just is. Homosexuality is as natural to homosexuals as heterosexuality is to heterosexuals. And how can we expect people to change their identity? How can *God* expect those *he* has oriented toward homosexuality to go against their nature?

Although most Christians don't condone homosexual activity, they have been affected by the homosexual agenda enough to believe that there is some sort of homosexual orientation. The Ramsey Colloquium, a group of Jewish and Christian scholars, certainly agree.

> Although we are equal before God, we are not born equal in terms of our strengths and weaknesses, our tendencies and dispositions, our nature and nurture. We cannot utterly change the hand we have been dealt by inheritance and family circumstances, but we are responsible for how we play that hand.[8]

8 "Morality and homosexuality," *The Wall Street Journal,* 24 February 1994, 3.

Even well-known evangelicals have been sympathetic to this idea.[9] But we must be very careful at this point because the consequences are profound. For example, if you permit the idea of sinless homosexual orientation, you will encourage the church to look constantly for loopholes in the biblical data. After all, how can God hold people responsible who never choose to be homosexuals? Isn't homosexuality God's decision? The church cannot live with the idea of a natural homosexual orientation without, at some point, altering Scripture to fit our sense of God's character. The very least that will happen is that the church will back away from the severe warnings of Scripture, such as "homosexuals cannot inherit the kingdom of God" (1 Cor. 6:10). Such a warning sounds too harsh for people who are broken and need healing (in contrast to sinners who need repentance).

A second result of accepting a homosexual orientation (while frowning on homosexual behavior) is that the best counsel we can give someone with that orientation is, "Look but don't touch. You will always think it and want it, but don't actually *do* homosexual behavior." The victims of such counsel will never have the privilege of battling and rooting out sin at the level of the imagination. And eventually they will feel justified in being angry at God for giving them an orientation they may not live out.

The issue of homosexual orientation is where the church must engage the homosexual community in biblical discussion. The problem, however, is that the idea of homosexual orientation does not rest on any foundation that can be discussed. It relies on neither biblical data nor medical research. Instead, it is a political premise for gaining homosexual rights and is rooted in personal experience. Therefore, nei-

---

9 For example, Tony Campolo, "A Christian Sociologist Looks at Homosexuality," *The Wittenburg Door,* October–November 1977, 16–17. Also, T. Evans, "Homosexuality: Christian Ethics and Psychological Research," *Journal of Psychology and Theology* 3 (1975): 94–98.

ther biblical data nor refutation of the medical literature will persuade most homosexual advocates. Ultimately, most homosexuals appeal to their own feelings and the experience of their homosexual brothers and sisters. "Homosexuality feels right to us, so it is natural. It is part of our created constitution." But that should not keep us from examining their arguments biblically and engaging them in as much careful discussion as they are willing.

From a biblical perspective, it is possible that some Old Testament passages on homosexuality were intended, in part, to distance the Israelites from the practices of the Canaanites. One of those practices may have been male prostitution that was part of Canaanite religion (Deut. 23:17–18). This "unnatural" homosexuality *was* condemned. But is this the only kind of homosexual activity that is condemned?

If the Old Testament prohibitions were focused exclusively on cultic prostitution, why would the New Testament continue the prohibitions? The New Testament church was not focused on distancing itself from Canaanite religions. The church did, however, want to demonstrate God's holiness in its sexual behavior so that it would distance itself from the general licentiousness of the culture.

The idea that Leviticus spoke solely of male prostitution would be an unprecedented departure from the general tone of the biblical sexual prohibitions. Many of the Levitical laws were similar to those of the surrounding nations, but the Israelite codes consistently were morally *stronger* and more refined than those of pagan nations. For example, unchastity was punished more severely, and prostitution was illegal rather than regulated. Given the generally negative attitudes toward homosexual acts in places such as Egypt, Assyria, and Babylon,[10] it would be completely out of character for the Old Testament law to

10 D. Sherwin Bailey, *Homosexuality and the Western Christian Tradition* (London: Longmans, Green & Co., 1955).

prohibit homosexuality associated with idol worship while permitting it for other purposes. Furthermore, even if a passage such as Leviticus 18:22 did have cultic prostitution in mind, the fact that homosexuality was associated with cultic prostitution would make homosexuality in general all the more abhorrent.[11]

What about the other use of the term "unnatural"? Is it possible that the biblical texts were ignorant about homosexual orientation and were thus prohibiting only "unnatural" homosexual practice by participants of *heterosexual* orientation? This would suggest that the practicing homosexuals in the Bible were involved in homosexuality against their natural inclinations. Yet the nature of sin is that people sin because they *want* to sin (James 1:13–15). It comes from our desires. No one is dragged into sin kicking and screaming. Homosexuality existed in biblical times because people enjoyed it; they were drawn to it by their own hearts (Mark 7:21–23). An artificial distinction between (sinful) homosexual practice and (justifiable) homosexual orientation contradicts the Scripture's constant connection of desire, orientation, and deed. If the deed was prohibited in Scripture, the desire was too.

For homosexuals who are committed to thinking biblically, this may *begin* to challenge their ideas on homosexual orientation. But a very significant question remains: Why does it feel natural? The biblical answer is relatively straightforward. Like many other sins, homosexuality does not have to be learned. The child who never witnessed a temper tantrum can be proficient at throwing them; it is an instinctive ability of the human heart. Homosexuality is natural in the same way that anger or selfishness is natural. They are embedded in

---

11 Greg Bahnsen also notes, "Parallel reasoning would lead us to deem bestiality [mentioned in Leviticus 12:23] outside of religious or cultic contexts as morally acceptable—a conclusion that ought to shock our ethical sensibilities." In *Homosexuality: A Biblical View* (Grand Rapids: Baker, 1978), 45.

our fallen humanness. Indeed, homosexuality is "natural," but only in the sense that it is an expression of the sinful nature.

The fact that most homosexuals cannot remember consciously choosing homosexuality is also readily explained by Scripture. Most sin works on a level where we do not self-consciously choose it. To use Old Testament language, our sin can be "unintentional," but that does not make us less responsible for our violation of God's will (Lev. 5:14–19; Num. 15:22–30). Sin is more than mature, rational, conscious decisions. It is our moral inclination from birth.

Are the Biblical Prohibitions Relevant to Committed Homosexual Relationships?

Some may respond, "Isn't the issue really love? Aren't casual, unloving sexual relationships what Scripture prohibits?" As one proponent has said, "The church must take a very open attitude to various sexual orientations and various forms of human relationships ... as long as these are conducted in a loving and responsible way."[12]

But that would imply that the biblical prohibitions are unclear, and that an appeal must be made to the clearer law of love. Yet the Leviticus passages seem explicit. Leviticus 18:22 states, "Do not lie with a man as one lies with a woman." No exception is made for their loyalty to or love for each other. The sexual act itself is condemned, not just the attitude of the offender. Leviticus 20:12 reads in a similar way, but it includes the punishment for homosexual relations: "Their blood will be on their own heads." The severity of the punishment stresses the moral nature of the act.

Advocates of the homosexual hermeneutic raise various objections. "Isn't it still possible that the writers of Scripture simply did not

12 A. Dostourian, "Gayness: A Radical Christian Approach," in L. Crew, ed., *The Gay Academic* (Palm Springs: ETC, 1978), 347.

know of committed homosexual relationships? After all, the prejudice against homosexuality was intense, leaving homosexuals with little opportunity for committed relationships."

Such an argument suggests that the Old Testament was naive about sexual relations. A quick reading of Leviticus 18–20, however, would indicate otherwise. While the details of the sexual practices of the Old Testament times are unclear, the sheer number of prohibitions suggests that the breadth of sexual possibilities is not a recent phenomenon. Furthermore, the sexual practices of New Testament times are more available to us than those of the Old, and it is certain that the Greek and Roman cultures had every kind of homosexuality imaginable. Yet the apostle Paul, in keeping with the Old Testament, offers no exceptions to the prohibitions against homosexuality.

It is true that, on some level, there can be great affection and commitment in a homosexual relationship. But this doesn't mean that the relationship is approved by God. If a man is unbiblically divorced and marries a woman he believes he truly loves, that union is still wrong. Adulterous relationships may, on some level, be loving and committed, but they also are still wrong.

Many homosexuals agree with these analogies. Someone—the nonadulterous spouse—is victimized by adultery. But what about love and loyalty when no one else seems to be hurt, such as premarital sexual relationships?

Such an argument does not apprehend biblical love. Love is not simply the absence of obvious injury to anyone. For example, critical thoughts don't victimize, but they are unloving and wrong. Defining love in terms of whether people get hurt misses the heart of biblical teaching.

We may not autonomously decide what form love takes. God tells us how to love. When we love on *our* terms rather than his, we are in sin. Even if our sin does not seem to hurt another human being, it is still sin. If sin were reduced to hurting others, then we could become morally perfect by isolating ourselves from all people. Sin, however, is not primarily a human-against-human action. It is human-against-God. God defines love as obedience to him.

Have Biblical Prohibitions of Homosexuality Expired with Old Testament Ceremonial Codes?

Another objection raised by homosexuals is that these Levitical prohibitions are ceremonial, enforced only during a specific period in Israel's history. Like the laws declaring certain animals unclean, the laws against homosexuality are no longer applicable. This is untenable, however, for the two reasons already mentioned. First, the penalty for violation was death, which was the penalty for moral violations rather than violations of ceremonial law. Second, the New Testament writers considered the laws to be applicable.

Do the Prohibitions Come from Other Mandates That Are No Longer Relevant?

A fourth objection to the permanence of the command against homosexuality is that it was written to a culture under the weight of the mandate to fill the earth and subdue it. Homosexuality, because it produces no offspring, would not be politically correct in such an environment. With the coming of Christ, some suggest, the mandate was rightly interpreted as a command to evangelize. It called for a spiritual filling more than a procreative filling. Furthermore, in a world that seems somewhat cramped, there is no longer a need to emphasize the procreative aspect of the mandate.

This argument may seem like grasping at straws at first, but parts of it would likely appeal to most Christians. For instance, how many people use birth control? Does that violate the commandment to fill the earth? Or what about married couples who choose to be childless? Are such people excommunicated? How does a homosexual union differ from a heterosexual union that is childless, whether by choice or barrenness?

This kind of homosexual argument might have merit if the purpose of marriage were simply procreation. But that is not the sole purpose of marriage. Marriage is a covenant of companionship ordained by God. It is the one-flesh union of two people who are truly "fit" for each other. It is not deficient or immoral when the marriage is barren, but it is immoral if there is a violation of the marital design.

This takes us back again to the question of the validity of committed, loving, homosexual relationships. Aren't these also covenants of companionship? How can we say that two people of the same sex who love each other can't enjoy the privilege of marital sexuality? Again, we emphasize that God defines the way we love each other.

The Biblical Position

Before leaving this very brief biblical discussion, we should remember that all of us can twist Scripture to justify anything we do. Our hearts enjoy sin and we are quick to self-justify and self-deceive. We search for biblical permission to follow our own desires and quiet the rumblings of our conscience.

Is it possible that the church is self-deceived? Is it possible that we are sinfully homophobic and looking for biblical warrant for our prejudice? It is possible. Our response should be prayerfully to search our own hearts and Scripture. This, I trust, is what I have done.

Is it also possible that homosexuals are self-deceived because they want their own desires more than obedience to God? Is it possible that, like good defense lawyers, they are trying to plant a seed of doubt so that they can liberate their consciences and practice their desires? This possibility should be taken especially seriously. The homosexual hermenuetic disagrees with a plain reading of Scripture, goes contrary to the history of biblical interpretation,[13] and is reminiscent of the Pharisaic narrowing of the law so condemned in the New Testament.

The biblical position is that there is a creation order for human sexuality. God's ordained design for sexual relationships is male-female. Homosexual acts *and* homosexual *desires,* male or female, violate this creation ordinance and are thus sinful. The church must therefore warn and rebuke those who call themselves Christians but persist in homosexual practice. *And* the church must actively teach that homosexual *affection* is sinful. It can never suggest that there is a morally neutral, constitutional, homosexual orientation. To urge those struggling with homosexual desire simply to refrain from acting on their desire is to sin against these brothers and sisters.

Biological Causes of Homosexuality

Having reviewed the biblical arguments, we can more confidently let Scripture assert itself and provide clear oversight of the brain research. What we would expect to find in the research is this: careful scientific observations will harmonize with the biblical position. *Interpretations* of that research may differ from the biblical perspective, but the observations themselves, assuming they are reliable, will not. And this indeed is the case: the findings of science support rather than challenge the biblical view.

Perhaps the best known study on the biology of homosexuality ap-

---

13 Some have suggested that while the history of the church has not approved of homosexual relationships, it has not always opposed them. James B. Nelson, "Sources for Body Theology: Homosexuality as a Test Case," in Jeffrey Siker, ed., *Homosexuality in the Church* (Louisville: Westminster John Knox Press, 1994), 76–90.

peared in the periodical *Science*.[14] The lead researcher, Simon LeVay, conducted post-mortem examinations on the brains of nineteen homosexual men who died from AIDS and sixteen presumed heterosexual men, six of whom died of AIDS. His results suggested that the brains of the heterosexual men consistently had more brain cells in a specific area of the brain (INAH 3) that is allegedly implicated in sexual behavior. When viewed with a homosexuality-as-biologically-determined bias, the data show that homosexuality is located in the brain.

Christians and non-Christians have often noted that this study in no way establishes a causal link between brain activity and homosexual behavior. Even LeVay concedes the limitations of his study, suggesting that it is little more than an invitation to further research. He knows that his observations are very tentative until corroborated by other researchers, and this corroboration has not yet been forthcoming. He recognizes that AIDS may have confounded the results, that the sample size was too small to draw any clear conclusions, and that his measurements could be prone to error. Furthermore, the brains of three homosexual men in the study were indistinguishable from the analogous brain areas in heterosexual men. Even his assumption that there is a relationship between INAH 3 and sexual behavior has never been clearly established.

Therefore, we can conclude very little from this study. But what if eventually there is research that avoids the weaknesses of this study and actually establishes some connection between the size of INAH 3 and homosexuality? Even then, LeVay acknowledges that "the results do not allow one to decide if the size of INAH 3 in an individual is the cause or the consequence of that individual's sexual orientation." In

---

14 Simon LeVay, "A Difference in Hypothalamic Structure Between Heterosexual and Homosexual Men," *Science* 253 (1991): 1034–37.

other words, from his perspective the possible brain differences may just as likely *result from* homosexuality as cause it.

Or let's take the most extreme possibility. Though this could never happen in this generation because of the potential methodological problems inherent in such research, imagine that someone were able to demonstrate that INAH 3 is indeed a factor in sexual desire, and that INAH 3 is smaller *from birth* in people who eventually become homosexuals. In other words, the neuronal patterns in the brain do not *result* from homosexual experience; the smaller INAH 3 *precedes* homosexual activity.

If such research existed, Christians (and many non-Christians) could make at least the following observations: First, there would always be exceptions to the rule. Some heterosexuals would have a smaller INAH 3, and some homosexuals would have a larger INAH 3. Second, even the secular writers would insist, as they do now, that biology is not destiny. Human sexual response is too complex to be reduced to a neuron deficit in the brain. Third, Christians would remain firm in their stance that biology can't make us sin. At most, biology is analogous to a friend who tempts us into sin. Such a friend might be bothersome, but he can be rebuked and resisted.

Another approach to studying the biological basis of homosexuality is to observe the incidence of homosexuality in families and twins. A favorite example is the research done by Michael Bailey and Richard Pillard.[15] This study reported that of fifty-six homosexual men who were identical twins, 52 percent (twenty-nine) had a twin brother who was also homosexual. Among nonidentical twins the rate was 22 percent; among nontwin brothers the rate was 9 percent, and among adopted siblings the rate was 11 percent. The research group also

---

15 J. Michael Bailey and Richard C. Pillard, "A Genetic Study of Male Sexual Orientation," *Archives of General Psychiatry* 48 (1991): 1089–97.

found comparable statistics with females.[16] This is what you would expect if there were a genetic component to homosexuality: the closer the genetic relationship, the higher the rate of shared homosexuality.

However, this study, like LeVay's, produces no firm conclusions. Even if you ignore the sampling biases (they recruited through homosexual publications) and the fact that no other researchers outside this team have found such high percentages among identical twins, the study is inconsequential. That is because identical twins typically have a profound influence on each other. If one twin is introduced to something new, it is likely that he will introduce the other twin to that activity. Moreover, why did genetically unrelated, adopted brothers of homosexuals have such an allegedly high rate of homosexuality? Their 11 percent incidence rate was five times what you would expect. (The incidence of active homosexuality is generally believed to be about 2 percent in the general population.[17]) The study would be better used to support the influence of peers in the development of homosexuality.

The researchers realize that all they have proved is that homosexuality is *not* caused solely by genetics. If genetics were the only cause, the concordance rate in identical twins would be 100 percent. If one twin were homosexual, the other twin—having identical genes— would *always* be homosexual. Since the statistic is much lower than that, homosexuality cannot be a straightforward genetic trait. Apart from this conclusion, the study is not able to prove anything. Along with problems in the way the study was structured, identical twins share an environment that is more similar than that of other siblings. Therefore, it is not unusual for them to share behavior. The only way

16 J. Michael Bailey et al., "Heritable Factors Influence Sexual Orientation in Women," *Archives of General Psychiatry* 50 (1993): 217–24.

17 John O. Billy et al., "The Sexual Behavior of Men in the United States," *Family Planning Perspectives* 25 (1993): 52–61.

to strengthen such research would be to study twins who were separated at birth.

But imagine, again, that this research were supported by better studies that were consistently replicated. What if research found that identical twins more frequently share homosexuality even when they have no contact with each other? If this research were to emerge, it would still illustrate biblical truth. First, there will never be a 100 percent concordance rate. Second, a principle of Scripture is that the context for our lives is the physical body, and we should expect that the physical body (the brain in this case) would have some way to represent biologically the intents of the heart. For example, people who have a habit of sinful anger demonstrate different patterns of brain activity than do those who are very peaceful because of faith in Christ. Such an observation does not mean that the brain *makes* us angry. It simply means that the brain can display the physical etchings of the intents of the heart.

Let's go one step further. In the case of homosexuality, it is even possible that a certain brain type is *necessary* to express homosexual intent. Nevertheless, this brain or genetic hardware is not *sufficient* to cause homosexuality.

Am I now suggesting that it is biblically possible for the body to cause homosexuality? Indeed, I am, provided—and read carefully—the word "cause" in this context means "biologically shape or influence," *not* "irresistibly compel." Used this way, there is nothing shocking about what I am saying. Our sinful hearts express themselves in behavior via hundreds of factors, biology being one. A person whose sinful heart acts out in murder may have been influenced by unjust treatment, by parents who allowed him to vent his rage on siblings, and by Satan's incessant suggestions to kill. But none of these influences remove his personal responsibility for his intentions or actions. The ultimate cause of sin is always the sinful heart.

To use the more scientific terms of *necessary* and *sufficient,* biology may be *necessary* for some homosexuality, but biology is not a *sufficient* cause in and of itself. Consider the following illustration. If I am going to wash my car, I will need a pail of water. A bucket of soapy water will be *necessary.* If I don't have it, I won't be able to wash the car. Of course, there are a number of other necessary conditions that must be in place if I am to wash my car, such as good weather, available time, and a dirty car. None of these conditions, however, is *sufficient* for the task of washing the car. That is, none of them can irresistibly force me to wash it. The *sufficient* condition for me to wash the car is that—in addition to all the necessary conditions—I have the intention or motivation to wash it. I must *want* to wash the car.[18] In the case of homosexuality, the sufficient condition is the function of the heart, and that is something for which I am always responsible.

A third type of research on the biological basis of homosexuality also focuses on genetic data—this time not in large populations, but at the microscopic level, in the gene itself. The best known of the research teams doing this work is from the National Institute of Health and is headed by Dean Hamer.[19] This highly technical work is in its infancy, but neither its youth nor its sophistication should keep the Christian lay person from asserting the functional authority of Scripture over the data.

As in the two studies previously mentioned, there are methodological flaws in this study, and the results have only been duplicated by Hamer's team (with statistics that are not as impressive as the first study). So there is really very little that must be said at this point. Even

---

18 When I was younger, my father *made* me wash the car, often against my desires. This, however, is not analogous to the homosexual experience. It is analogous to sexual abuse.

19 Dean H. Hamer et al., "A Linkage Between DNA Markers on the X Chromosome and Male Sexual Orientation," *Science* 261 (1993): 321–27.

if practicing homosexuals were consistently genetically distinct from heterosexuals, this would not make homosexuality a biologically based behavior for which people bear no moral responsibility. Biology is not the sufficient, determinative cause of biblically prohibited behavior. Our desire to practice it is.

These three studies are the most recent in a relatively long but fruitless attempt to discover whether homosexuality is biologically determined. One physician who reviewed the literature said, "Recent studies postulate biologic factors as the primary basis for sexual orientation. However, there is no evidence at present to substantiate a biologic theory, just as there is no evidence to support any singular psychosocial explanation."[20] The only thing certain is that human sexuality is too complex to be reduced to the workings of the brain.

It is true that the brain can cause certain behaviors. It can cause hallucinations, disordered thinking, and speech difficulties—all behaviors that would be labeled as weaknesses. But it can't cause sin. Therefore, it would be surprising to hear of future studies that offer better evidence for a biology-causes-homosexual-behavior link. If they do, they will send us back to the theological drawing boards to see if we are correctly apprehending Scripture's view of the mind-body relationship. At this point, however, Scripture seems clear, and the actual scientific observations offer no resistance to biblical oversight.

A Biblical Model of Homosexuality

While the church has been quick to refute the biologic literature, it has been slow to apply the same principles to the psychological theories. For various reasons, we tend to be more comfortable with psychological influences than biological ones. For example, a popular the-

---

20 William Byne and Bruce Parsons, "Homosexual Orientation: The Biologic Theories Reappraised," *Archives of General Psychiatry* 50 (1993): 228–39.

ory is that almost all homosexuality, male or female, is a deficit in the relationship with the same-sex parent. The theory is that there is a God-designed need for same-sex love, affirmation, acceptance, and bonding. When these allegedly normal attachment needs have been left unmet, the needs become eroticized at puberty. Homosexuality is a drive to make good this relationship.

When we listen closely to the application of this and other psychological explanations,[21] it looks as if the church, while barricading the front door to keep out the brain theories, has left open the back door for the psychological theories. The reason for this omission is clear. The church wants to emphasize that homosexuality is learned rather than biologically inbred; and since it is learned, it can be unlearned. But notice the problem. All this does is suggest that the orientation toward homosexuality starts a little after birth instead of before birth. We are left at almost the same place as the biological theories: the orientation is still established by forces outside of ourselves, and orientation precedes sin (Figure 9.2). This reasoning infers that the real problem, the deep problem, is a homosexual orientation for which we are not responsible. A diagnosis of sin and a cure that includes repentance would be considered superficial.

A biblical view acknowledges that there may be psychological and biological influences in the development of homosexuality. In fact, the Bible would warn us not to take lightly the vast number of possible influences. However, Scripture states adamantly that such influences are not what make us "unclean." Instead, "from within, out of men's hearts, come evil thoughts, sexual immorality. . . . All these evils come from inside and make a man 'unclean' " (Mark 7:21–23;

21 Others have suggested that homosexuality is a result of victimization. For example: E. Hurst and D. Jackson, *Overcoming Homosexuality* (Elgin, Ill.: David C. Cook, 1987), Leanne Payne, *A Broken Image* (Westchester, Ill.: Crossway, 1981), and *Crisis in Masculinity* (Westchester, Ill.: Crossway, 1985).

PRIMARY CAUSE	SECONDARY CAUSE	RESPONSE
biology, or deficit in relationship with same-sex parent, low self-esteem, and so on →	sin →	homosexuality

Figure 9.2. A common, unbiblical view of the development of homosexuality

SUFFICIENT CAUSE	POSSIBLE NECESSARY INFLUENCES	SINFUL PRACTICE
sinful heart →	genetics, peers, family, sexual violation by an → older person, and so on	homosexuality

Figure 9.3. The development of homosexuality

see Figure 9.3). This means that our sinful orientation has innumerable expressions in our lives. With some people it is greed or jealousy, with others it is sinful anger, and with others it can be expressed in homosexual desire.

The Process of Change

Like all sin, homosexuality at the level of the heart's desires does not relent easily or quickly. It is put to death over time. But change is certainly possible through progressive sanctification. "Such were some of you" (1 Cor. 6:11) is the crucial reminder that there is hope to vanquish both homosexual acts *and* homosexual desire. How does this happen? The way of change is familiar. You need no special techniques. It consists of simultaneously juggling two themes: the knowledge of ourselves and the knowledge of God. When counseling a homosexual, present these two themes in a spirit of love and with a willingness to listen.

173

Listening is a good place to start. After all, how can we bring truth to a person unless we know him? So you might begin with questions. What is it like to struggle with homosexuality? What are some of the events that shaped the present expression of homosexuality? Salient past events may need to be addressed. Was the person homosexually raped? Was he or she manipulated into sexual activity by an older person? This victimization doesn't explain homosexuality, and it doesn't mean that people are not responsible for their future thoughts and actions. But God certainly speaks with compassion to those who have been sinned against, and homosexuals must hear this.[22] How has the person been hurt in relationships? How has it been painful to pursue a homosexual lifestyle? What is it like to be confronted suddenly with having to leave close friends, long-term partners, or a supportive community? "I ached physically from all the emotional turmoil," said a man who was leaving his partner. "But several Christian heterosexual men made themselves available any time of the day or night. I'm alive today because those guys loved me."[23]

In this context, we should introduce the knowledge of God, especially God's forgiveness of sinners. This is the anthem that both attracts and changes those struggling with homosexuality.

Some people believe that there is already enough teaching that God warmly embraces everyone, and not enough about God's justice and hatred of sin. This may be true, but it is no reason to sacrifice the greatness of the doctrine of grace. Homosexuals are in a complex position: they are rebels against a holy God, but they are also, at some level, aware of their sin and afraid of God's wrath (Rom. 1). They do not believe that God could really bring himself to forgive them. As C. John Miller has said, "There is no more important factor in the

22 See my article on suffering, "Exalting Pain? Ignoring Pain? What Do We Do with Suffering?" *Journal of Biblical Counseling* 12 (spring 1994).
23 Bob Davies, "Will We Offer Hope?," *Moody*, May 1994, 16.

transforming of a homosexual than the confident faith that his or her sins really have been pardoned by God at their deepest root."[24]

To know the grace of forgiveness, homosexuals must know the truth about themselves: they are sinners in need of grace. Even though they have some knowledge of this, they often lack biblical clarity because their knowledge of sin is suppressed. The flesh does not want to see sin in all its ugliness; it works to keep it covered. What clouds sin even more is the myth that there is, by God's design, a homosexual orientation. These two factors work violently against the truth about ourselves.

The process of exposing the heart comes through the Holy Spirit's application of Scripture. The goal is to understand what God says, to learn to "think God's thoughts." One way into Scripture is to understand that there actually *is* something deeper than homosexuality. As summarized in Romans 1, homosexuality is an expression of an idolatrous heart. *This* is our deepest problem. We have an instinct that switches our allegiance from God to our idols. What are our idols? Comfort, pleasure, power, personal meaning, self-esteem, and so on. The possibilities are endless, but they all have one thing in common: an allegiance to self. We rebel against God, and we choose to live for our glory rather than God's. We choose to obey our own desires rather than God's Word. Homosexual desire or activity is an expression of the idolatrous instincts of our hearts.

Does the person have questions about homosexual orientation? Does he (or she) have a sense that he was always more interested in same-sex relationships? If so, stick with this issue until the person can think biblically about it. It is too easy to settle for the absence of homosexual behavior and not worry about attitudes. Remember that it is on the question of homosexual orientation that the world,

24 C. John Miller, "The Gay '80s," *Eternity,* November 1986, 18.

the flesh, and the Devil converge. The world, with its sub-biblical views, has voted that homosexuality is normal. Our flesh wants to exonerate itself from homosexual fantasy and maintain that sexual gratification is a sacred right. And the Devil stands behind both, whispering his murderous deceptions. The deception of homosexual orientation must be exposed and corrected. It is a false teaching that will eventually lead to bad fruit. We truly do have an "orientation," but it is a spiritual orientation that is against God. It is not a simple physical propensity.

As the Holy Spirit exposes these critical issues about a person, the Spirit also reveals more of the knowledge of God. The theme of God's love continues, but now we are reminded that it is a *holy* love. By holy we mean that it is unparalleled in human experience. There is nothing like it. It is beyond comprehension and it is unsurpassed. It is a love distinct or separate from our own. As a result it leaves witnesses in awe. This is the beginning of the fear of the Lord. When we witness his forgiveness, we learn the fear of the Lord (Ps. 130:4). When the disciples saw his power over the wind and the waves, "they were terrified" and grew in the fear of the Lord (Mark 4:41). When Isaiah was taken into the throne room, he was so overwhelmed by the holiness of God that he cried out, "I am ruined" (Isa. 6:5). Isaiah's knowledge of God's holy majesty and holy forgiveness established him in the fear of the Lord for the rest of his ministry as a prophet. Indeed, the fear of the Lord is both the beginning of wise living and its goal.

One of the great blessings of the fear of the Lord is that it can teach us to hate sin (Prov. 8:13). The knowledge of the holy can mobilize. It can take the drudgery out of daily self-control. It can make us warriors against the tendencies of our sinful nature. This aggressive stance toward sin is especially critical since our problem is that we *like* it. It has the power of our affections. If we don't root out these affections, we are guaranteed that temptation will be nearly overpowering. The fear of the Lord can keep us battle-ready. With the heavenly throne in sight, we do battle with the "sin that so easily entangles" (Heb. 12:1).

Therefore I do not run like a man running aimlessly; I do not fight like a man beating the air. No, I beat my body and make it my slave so that after I have preached to others, I myself will not be disqualified for the prize. (1 Cor. 9: 26–27)

. . . let us run with perseverance the race marked out for us. Let us fix our eyes on Jesus. . . . (Heb. 12:1–2)

What expectations should there be for change? What is the goal? The goal, again, is to think God's thoughts rather than our own. This means that we can engage the battle when we see the very *seeds* of homosexual temptation (James 1:13–15). We can grow to be able to hate anything that hints of rebellion against God. We can be liberated from homosexual obsession. And we can understand that male-female marriage is one of God's good gifts. This does not mean that all people who once struggled with homosexuality will pursue marriage. In some cases, God gives grace to be celibate. In contrast to the common idea that this is a fate worse than death, celibacy can promote "undivided devotion to the Lord" (1 Cor. 7:35). It can be a blessing, not a curse. But since marriage is a good gift, and God's pleasure is toward Christian marriage, then as one-time homosexuals grow in adopting the mind of Christ, they will find pleasure in the same thing that God does.

How long will it take? If a person is willing to follow Christ and he or she is surrounded by a caring church, homosexual behavior can stop immediately. "The grace of God . . . teaches us to say 'No' to ungodliness and worldly passions, and to live self-controlled, upright and godly lives . . ." (Titus 2:11–12). No one should think, however, that homosexual *desire* will be gone as quickly. The person who has had a long history of homosexual practice will be doing battle for many years. The power of homosexual thoughts to enslave will gradually be defeated, but the stray homosexual thought may be evident decades after there has been cessation of homosexual acts. Is this discouraging? No, it means that God is at work, giving power to fight, reminding us that warfare is normal, progressively sanctifying us, and giving us the privilege of constantly depending on Christ by faith.

To make steady progress toward these goals, one-time homosexuals need more than a counselor. Like us all, they need the larger body of Christ and its varied relational opportunities. Men need other men who love, listen, and model brotherly relationships. Women need other women with whom they can have close but not obsessive or sexualized relationships. Both men and women need elders and pastors who can faithfully pray, and, if necessary, bring church discipline as a means of God's loving correction. Other relationships might include small groups with couples and singles, accountability groups with other men, and small prayer groups. In some cases, churches may have specialized ministries to homosexuals (e.g., support groups) or more general ministries to those who want to leave sexual slavery of any kind.

Does this mean that homosexual persons can be members of the Christian church? It is important to be biblically careful with this question. Consider a person who, at a membership interview, professes the name of Christ and indicates that he or she has stopped homosexual activity but is still struggling with homosexual temptation. Furthermore, suppose the person professes a clear commitment, by God's grace, to fight against this sin at the level of the imagination. Such a person would not accurately be described as a homosexual and would be welcomed into the nurturing arms of the church. If, however, the question refers to an avowed practicing homosexual joining the church, then the church would refuse admission and, instead, pursue the person in love in order to lead him or her to repentance.

What if a member of the church is found to be practicing homosexuality? Most churches have guidelines for the discipline of such a brother or sister that specify how the principles of Matthew 18:15–20 are applied. Sadly, these guidelines are often ignored. What results is a person whose soul is in peril because church leaders have not pursued God's means of reconciliation. To withhold church discipline, even discipline that proceeds to excommunication, would be to sin against the practicing homosexual.[25]

An effective church should *attract* homosexuals! That is, because of the love of Christ, the church should *pursue* them. And through its exaltation of Christ in preaching, corporate prayer, and worship, the church should attract them. It should also minister the Word to homosexuals in its midst by flushing out the self-deceived, exposing the dishonest, confronting the rebel, offering forgiveness to the guilt-ridden, and giving hope. The church should also welcome and draw the attention of those who struggle with homosexuality but have never been part of the church. It should minister by surprising such people with love, a sense of family, and the absence of self-righteous judgment. It should offer truth in such a way that is convicting, winsome, and radically different from anything else the homosexual has ever heard.

If you have a friend involved in homosexuality, you will likely learn a lot about yourself. Biblical dialogue begins with personal repentance. Before confronting sin in others, we must search out the sin resident in our own lives. Following the guidelines in Matthew 7:1–5, we are to allow the Spirit to expose our own hearts until we see that our sin is

---

25 See, e.g., John White and Ken Blue, *Healing the Wounded* (Downers Grove, Ill.: InterVarsity, 1985). Also, Jay Adams, *Handbook of Church Discipline* (Grand Rapids: Zondervan, 1986).

the same as that of the homosexual. Applying this biblical principle can be disarming to someone looking for a fight: it is difficult to argue with someone who is spiritually humble. Yet, sadly, although the theory is clear, the practice is difficult and uncommon.

Many Christians admit that they are sinners but don't see their sin in quite the same category as homosexuality. Homosexuality, being a sin "against nature," is perceived to be abnormal even among sins. Heterosexuals are often mystified by same-sex attractions. Christians can see in their hearts the seed of most other sins, but few can even imagine being tempted by homosexuality. Yet homosexuality comes from the same heart that generates greed, envy, strife, disobedience to parents, and gossip (Rom. 1:29–32).

With repentant and humble spirits, we need to pursue those who practice homosexuality, and we need to do that without a hint of self-righteousness. Scripture condemns that kind of judgment, and homosexuals will be quick to detect it.

This personal repentance, however, is only the beginning of the preparation for dialogue. Because of our solidarity with those who call themselves Christians, there are corporate sins in which we share. Has the church been, at times, self-righteous in its attitude toward homosexuals? Is there homophobia in some of our congregations? Do we tend to think of homosexuality as worse than the gossip and private idolatries that are rampant in the church? Has the church been unwelcoming to unbelieving but spiritually searching homosexuals? The answer to these questions is certainly yes. More specifically, the answer is, "Yes, *we* have sinned."

But what if you personally have not sinned against a homosexual? Perhaps you have never even met someone involved in a homosexual lifestyle. Is corporate repentance appropriate even then? According to Daniel and Nehemiah, although we may not be personally guilty for some sins, we have a unity with others in the church. We therefore share in the sins of other Christians, and it is appropriate to confess them, as Daniel did:

> O Lord, the great and awesome God, who keeps his covenant of love with all who love him and obey his commands, we have sinned and done wrong. We have been wicked and rebelled; we have turned away from your commands and laws. We have not listened to your servants the prophets. . . . (Dan. 9:4–6)

This is the starting point in speaking with homosexuals: Allow others to point out your institutional sins. Ask how *the church* has sinned against homosexuals. Then, if you find even a kernel of truth in what is said, confess these sins, ask forgiveness, and invite the homosexual, in the name of Jesus, to talk with you further.

HOMOSEXUALITY is one area where Christians *have* provided biblical oversight of the brain and biological research. The debate has generated a number of good articles and books that have studied both the biblical texts and the brain research. Be alert, however, to the distinction that some make between homosexual desire and homosexual activity. This is an area where we may have been influenced by the *interpretations* of the brain research, while Scripture shines a much brighter, clearer light.

ALCOHOLISM

HOMOSEXUALITY was called sin for many years. In this century, especially since Freud's writings, it came to be seen as an abnormality. Even into the late 1970s, homosexuality was considered abnormal. Now, because of cultural pressures, the classification has changed again. Today, homosexuality is commonly thought to be a natural, brain-based variation of sexual expression.

Alcoholism has not traveled quite as far: it has only gone from sin to disease. Because of the horrible consequences of heavy drinking on both the drinker and the family, no one is willing to say it is normal. Yet there are very few who would say that the abuse of alcohol is sin or, at least, solely sin.

> A Gallup poll found that a great majority of Americans are convinced that alcoholism is indeed an illness rather than a sign of moral backsliding. In fact, they have the support of the American Medical Association, which twenty-one years ago formally declared alcoholism a disease.[1]

---

1 E. Desmond, "Out in the Open," *Time,* 30 November 1987, 87.

Christians know that there is a problem here. The Bible unequivo-cally states that drunkenness is sin; the popular vote says it is sickness. Has the Bible been wrong or pre-scientific in its analysis? Has it been *harmful* to alcoholics by stigmatizing them? For those who believe that the Bible speaks with authority and clarity to the issues of life, these questions must be answered. If you come to believe that alcoholism is a disease even though Scripture says it is something else, then your confidence in Scripture will erode. After all, if Scripture is out of date in understanding this problem, it may be out of date on many others as well.

Some people have tried to protect the doctrine of biblical inerrancy by suggesting that the drunkenness talked about in the Bible is some-thing completely different from the alcoholism of today. But this doesn't really help. It still leaves us asking, "What else doesn't the Bible address?" If we were wrong in thinking that it spoke clearly to drunk-enness and alcoholism when it actually doesn't, what will we find to-morrow that it doesn't really address? Will we have to change our thinking on everything we now call an addiction, such as being ruled by sex, food, or other drugs? Should *all* these problems be more ac-curately labeled diseases?

On the other hand, if the Bible *is* correct in its statements about drunkenness and alcoholism, what does that say about all the people who feel as if they have a disease? What does it say about all the med-ical research? When we dialogue about alcoholism, we are truly on the horns of a dilemma.

To work through these issues, I will take a slightly different ap-proach. Rather than dispassionately review the relevant exegetical and medical details, I will discuss them by way of a personal letter. In this way, I am remembering that we are attempting to help real peo-ple struggling with life-dominating problems. We are not just dealing with an abstract, academic issue.

A *Personal Letter*

Dear brothers and sisters,

I have never been an addict, at least not in the narrow sense. But I have known many addicts, and I have been changed by them. I have been taught by their willingness to ask for help, their openness with their struggles, and their desire to live one day at a time. These relationships have caused me to think a lot about addictions.

I have been especially interested in thinking about what causes addictions. How do we become addicts? Is it genetic? Is it caused by the brain? When does our brain make us do it, and when doesn't it? At first, I thought these questions were very interesting but not very relevant to the task of sobriety. But I have now learned that they are more than simply interesting. They are also very important. In fact, they get all the way to the ultimate questions of life, even to God himself.

I found this out over lunch one day.

"I am getting angry with God for giving me this problem with alcohol," my friend confided. "Most people in the world don't have to struggle to stay away from the next drink every day of their lives. But I do. It's just not fair."

I was stunned. My friend was judging God for what he believed was his genetic vulnerability to alcohol. Before he made that comment, I had been thinking how great it was that he wasn't drinking anymore. The way he actually understood his problem and the strategies he used to deal with it hadn't seemed that important. He was sober, and that was enough. But after his comment, I realized that his view of *how* he became an alcoholic was *very* important. Apparently, his theory put the blame (at least in part) on his brain, and since God made his brain, God shared responsibility for my friend's temptations and vulnerabilities.

Chapter Ten

Sin or Sickness? Two Views

There are essentially two views regarding alcoholism and most other addictions: a medical one and a moral or religious one. The medical view says that alcoholism is a disease; the moral view says it is sin or disobedience against God. Which view you accept has implications for the way you live your entire life.

As recently as the 1960s, most people agreed that alcohol abuse was sin—a problem of the heart—rather than a brain or chemical problem. Now the disease model dominates the public consciousness.

Has there been research evidence to justify this change? Not really (more on that later). The evidence is no greater than the evidence that homosexuality is caused by the brain. Then why is the disease model the most influential model today? There is one very powerful reason. The medical model dominates because the urge to drink *feels* like a disease. It *feels* like something else takes over when alcohol is available. For those who never struggled with it, it is easy to say that alcoholism is a self-conscious, immoral decision. But for those who experience it, it feels like anything but a decision. If there is a decision being made, it feels as if it is the disease that does the choosing.

The language of alcoholism captures this experience.

➤ "Treatment is best done in the hospital by professional medical personnel."

➤ "Once an alcoholic, always an alcoholic. There is no true cure."

➤ "One drink, one drunk."

➤ "That's the disease talking."

➤ "Medical treatments might soon be available."

➤ "You didn't choose this, so how could it be anything but a disease?"

This perspective is our culture's ruling metaphor on both the problem and the solutions. To deny it is to risk appearing foolish. And, since I'd rather not look like a fool, I would be glad to drop the whole matter. But I can't. For me, the issue is even greater than the fact that my friend made an unusual and troubling comment at lunch. The reason I can't drop the matter is because of the Bible. I believe that the Bible is God's roadmap for my life, and I believe that it understands—and speaks to—the inner workings of human beings better than anything else.

When we go to the Bible to see what it says about alcohol, there is one point that is hard to argue: the Bible always says that drunkenness is sin. The Bible uses illustrations (Gen. 9:18–27; 1 Kings 16:9), descriptions (Prov. 23:29–35), and prohibitions (1 Cor. 5:11; 6:9–10; Gal. 5:19–21) to emphasize that God says drunkenness is against his commands. No one who takes the Bible seriously has ever challenged this interpretation. However, there *are* different opinions about whether *drunkenness* in the Bible is really referring to modern *alcoholism* or substance abuse.

To compare these two concepts, let's first consider the modern definition of alcoholism or substance abuse. Here is how the experts define substance abuse:

A maladaptive pattern of substance use leading to clinically significant impairment or distress, as manifested by one (or more) of the following, occurring within a twelve-month period:

1. Recurrent substance use resulting in a failure to fulfill major role obligations at work, school, or home.
2. Recurrent substance use in situations in which it is physically hazardous.
3. Recurrent substance-related legal problems.

4. Continued substance use despite having persistent or recurrent social or interpersonal problems caused or exacerbated by the effects of the substance.[2]

Now, here is how the Bible describes drunkenness.

Who has woe? Who has sorrow?
   Who has strife? Who has complaints?
   Who has needless bruises? Who has bloodshot eyes?
Those who linger over wine,
   who go to sample bowls of mixed wine.
Do not gaze at wine when it is red,
   when it sparkles in the cup,
   when it goes down smoothly!
In the end it bites like a snake
   and poisons like a viper.
Your eyes will see strange sights
   and your mind imagine confusing things.
You will be like one sleeping on the high seas,
   lying on top of the rigging.
"They hit me," you will say, "but I'm not hurt!
   They beat me but I don't feel it!
When will I wake up
   so I can find another drink?" (Prov. 23:29–35)

Can you see that these descriptions are nearly identical? The main difference is that one is obviously more vivid than the other. The biblical description certainly illustrates the recurrent nature of drunkenness. It shows that the bad consequences are no deterrent to future

2 *Diagnostic Criteria from DSM-IV* (Washington, D.C.: American Psychiatric Association, 1994), 112.

excesses. Basically, there is no difference between the modern definition and the biblical description. When the Bible talks about drunkenness, it speaks to all the different experiences of alcohol abuse that
concern us today:

> the occasional weekend warrior who drinks too much while
watching football,

> the woman who can't get through the day without a brain-
numbing high,

> the obviously out-of-control person who persistently pursues
the beloved substance no matter what the consequences.

The point is this: we can't discount what the Bible says because we
think that it is unfamiliar with the modern problem of alcoholism. The
Bible is not naive about this painful, recurring problem. Like the disease model, it is very much aware that alcoholism feels like bondage.
It knows that change comes only by way of a fight and only with the
help of others. In fact, the biblical model intersects with the medical
one at a number of places. However, there is ultimately no confusing
the two. They each offer a particular way of understanding ourselves,
God, and the process of change.

The Disease Model: Cause and Cure

The disease model was first popularized by Bill Wilson, the founder
of Alcoholics Anonymous (AA), in the 1930s. A devoted pragmatist,
Wilson did not use the disease approach because it was well supported
by research; he used it because he thought it helped men and women
to be more open about their drinking problem. In other words, he was
using a metaphor: drinking is *like* a disease. Over the past fifty years,
however, the disease model has lost its metaphorical quality and it has

been shortened to "drinking *is* a disease." The disappearance of this little word *like* has made all the difference.

But there is more to the popular disease approach. If you have ever been to an AA meeting, you know that while the cause is always spoken of in disease terms, the cure is decidedly moral. There are no medications dispensed or surgeries to be had. You arrest the course of the disease by saying no. You both give up your will to a higher power and determine, with the help of others, to live an abstinent life. According to the AA tradition and the disease model, you are *not* responsible for the cause but you *are* responsible for the cure.

This apparent merging of the disease and moral models may seem unusual when put this way, but there is some precedent for it. For example, if you had juvenile diabetes, you are not responsible for the cause, but you are responsible for the cure in that you must watch your diet and faithfully take insulin. Or if you had kidney stones, you are not responsible for the cause, but you are responsible to drink lots of water and perhaps submit to surgery. But these examples are not quite the same as alcoholism or any other kind of addiction. With diabetes or kidney stones, the cure is outside ourselves. We have to rely on some procedure or medicine.

In alcoholism, however, the cure comes from within us. Of course, we may talk about God or a higher power as the cure, but there are many people—myself included—who believe that we must rely on God for *everything,* from driving a car to loving our wife. To say that we have to rely on someone other than ourselves does not mean that we have a physical disease. On the contrary. If the solution does not involve a technological or chemical corrective, that is strong evidence that the problem lies in the area of our choices and commitments, not our bodies or brains. It must. Otherwise abstinence would not be enough to tame the disease.

The Bible's Focus: Motivations and Desires

The Bible has a different view of how we first get involved in addictions. Instead of explaining the overpowering urge for alcohol as a disease, the Bible talks about our motivations and desires, forces so powerful that they can take over our lives. The Bible says that we first choose our addictions, and only then do our addictions choose us.

It is something like a marriage—a warped marriage. We enter it with all kinds of hopes and expectations. We like the way we feel when we are with our "partner" (alcohol). But then, once we really get into it, we learn more about the downside. The price of those good feelings is more than we bargained for. But by then, it is too late. We are committed to a way of life—stuck, if you really want to be honest. It isn't so easy anymore to leave our partner behind. And besides, there are times when it still *feels* good.... We'd miss those times, the ones that let us forget all the other times our partner has ruined things for us.

And so the addict goes back and forth, like a spouse in a bad marriage, sticking with the substance and trying to make the relationship work. On some days it is bad, and on others, not so bad. But it feels familiar, even comfortable—if you keep your expectations low enough.

What we've seen here is that there is a logic of sorts to alcohol abuse: we love drinking and what it does for us. We love it enough to be unwilling to do what it takes to remove it from our lives, despite its impact on our relationships and commitments. We may have moments of doubt and ambivalence, but ultimately we use it because we *want* to use it. We love it more than we care about any of the reasons to change.

[My wife] said to me that I was going to have to make a choice—either cocaine or her. Before she finished the sentence, I knew what was coming, so I told her to think carefully about what she was going to say. It was clear to me that there wasn't a choice. I love my wife, but I'm not going choose *anything* over cocaine. It's sick, but that's what things have come to. Nothing and nobody comes before my coke.[3]

Wouldn't you say that this man *loved* his cocaine? That he was controlled by his desires? "Don't ask me to make a choice," he says, "because I already know which object I love most." Isn't this something more than saying that he had an underlying disease? He *chose* the cocaine. He is just like the man who loves his mistress and leaves his wife. Does such a person have a genetically based sexual addiction that controls him? To make such a claim would be dehumanizing. We would be treating the adulterer like some animal who runs on instinct. We would be ignoring his motivations. We would be overlooking the fact that he is choosing the mistress because he wants to.

Of course, his choice is very shortsighted. He is not thinking at that moment that his children will hate him, that he will lose half his salary in alimony, and that his mistress won't look as good to him in six months. For him, the present is all that counts.

That is both the logic and the insanity of substance abuse. In fact, it seems to be the logic and insanity of the human condition. The infatuation of the moment rules us and we do things we later regret. By no means limited to drug and alcohol use, it is the same principle behind procrastination, buying on credit, eating too much dessert, spending all our money at the casino, and yelling at the boss. It may be incredibly unwise, but we care more about the way it makes us feel at the moment, and we wind up enslaved to the substances and behaviors that once brought us pleasure and release.

One weakness of a medical or disease approach to addictions is that

3 R. Weiss and S. Mirin, *Cocaine* (Washington, D.C.: American Psychiatric Association, 1987), 55.

it tends to minimize these motivations. While it certainly talks about our desires in some ways, its theory is that the ultimate cause for addiction is medical. This leaves us without a clear understanding of our wants, passions, and desires. And we need to understand these things because they are what drive us. Though the disease model does not ignore all of these motivations, it primarily directs our attention to possible biological causes. It does not offer the stark view of the human heart necessary to make deep changes.

God and Our Desires

The Bible's ability to get to the heart of the matter does not stop with its discussion of our desires. It goes one critical step further. It indicates that our temptations and lusts have much more to do with our relationship with God than we first think. In AA, even though God is part of The Twelve Steps and considered an essential help in getting out of addictions, heavy drinking is not considered an act against God. The reality, however, is that addictions are relational, or should I say they are anti-relational. Addictive behavior is against other people and even more so against God. We could put it this way: we love what our substance does for us more than we love God (or other people).

If we allow the Bible to reveal the unseen spiritual realities behind addictions, we suddenly realize that addictions are more than self-destructive behaviors. They are violations of God's laws: his laws that call us to avoid drunkenness and immoderate self-indulgence (Rom. 13:13), his law that calls us to love others (1 John 4:7), and his law that calls us to live for him rather than ourselves (1 Cor. 10:31). This means that addiction is more about someone's relationship with God than it is about biology. It reveals our allegiances: what we want, what we love, whom and what we serve. It brings us to that all-important question, "Will you live for the fulfillment of your desires or for God?"

The addiction-as-disease model misses this completely, and in some cases it can make the problem even worse. Consider again my friend who was angry with God. Rather than judging *himself* and asking how his behavior was against God, his disease model led him to judge God and accuse him of preferential or unfair treatment.

The Bible pushes us hard to face the Godward motivations that govern our choices. It argues that addictions reveal what or whom we *worship*. Will you worship your idols or will you worship God? From this perspective, a bottle of alcohol is one of many idols that we serve. It vies for our devotion along with money, pleasure, fame, sex, the opinions of others, and other popular idols of our time.

When we see the spiritual realities behind our addictive behaviors, we find that we serve what we *love*. Either we will love and serve God, or we will love and serve our idols. Idols exist in our lives because we love them and invite them in. But once idols find a home, they are unruly and resist leaving. In fact, they change from being the servants of our desires to being our masters. That is why the Bible says that we first choose the addictive substance, but then the addictive substance chooses us. We can either have the blessing of serving the Most High God who loves us, or we will have the curse of being a slave to our desires and the idols that symbolize them. That is why a biblical approach to addictions must do more than simply say, "Stop it." It realizes that addicts are both in control and out of control. This dual aspect of the addictive experience—the rebelliousness and the bondage—is what we commonly call *sin*, and it is a far deeper, more profound explanation of addictions than the disease metaphor.

The Deceitfulness of Sin

I have spoken to addictions groups where people have turned me off as soon as I said the word *sin*. I think I can understand why. When most people talk about sin, they are usually talking about a definite, self-conscious choice to do something wrong. The common though inaccurate view of sin is that a person wakes up in the morning and says, "Today I am going to sin. I am going to disobey God, hurt myself, hurt my spouse, and break promises to my children." Perhaps there is an addict who has said that, but I have never met him. That is simply not the typical experience of addictions.

Addiction doesn't feel like an attack against other people or rebellion against God. It feels more innocent—like a brief, potentially reversible decision just to give in a little bit to our own desires. But the word *sin* reminds us that it is not a small, temporary lapse. It reminds us that we are loving our desires (our idols), we are making choices to go against God, we are hurting other people, and we soon find ourselves in bondage. Sin is intentional, but it is also helplessness. It feels like a virus. It feels like a disease! But this experience doesn't take addictions out of the realm of sin. In fact, it illustrates the very nature of sin. Sin controls us. It captures and overtakes. In sin, we do things we don't want to do. This is the nature of all sin.

There is not a person in the world who has said no to sin and that was the end of it. If I see my selfishness in my relationship with my wife, I confess it and ask God to help me grow in love. I think I *have* grown in love over the years, but I still see my selfishness just as much now as I did fifteen years ago. Sin is stubborn. Even if a person can say no on a behavioral level, it is tougher to extinguish sin at the motivational level (the craving level). Why is it so tough? Because we are sinners. As sinners, we are shrewdly calculating *and* hopelessly out of control.

This is one reason why I can identify with the struggles of an addict. Even though I have not been an addict in the technical sense, I do possess the heart of an addict. I know what it is like to be a repeat offender. I can feel guilty about my sin, confess it, and then go right out and do it again. Drugs or alcohol don't make us addicts. They simply expose and attach themselves to the stuff that is already in every heart.

What About All the Evidence for Alcoholism as a Disease?

If I am right about sin and the heart, what do we do with all the evidence for alcoholism as a disease? Isn't the evidence beyond doubt? No, the evidence is not beyond doubt. In fact, *there is no clear evidence that alcoholism is primarily a disease.* Despite the many studies on alcoholism and drug abuse, none of them show that addictive behavior is clearly biological. No one has found a gene or a chemical imbalance. Most researchers are quick to point out that genes can *influence* people, and this of course is true. We can be genetically predisposed to enjoying a particular drug, food, or activity. But there is a huge difference between being influenced by genetics and being determined by it.

What about cravings? The Bible understands them well. It refers to them as temptations. The Bible recognizes that people with years of sobriety often still struggle with huge temptations. Sometimes this is just a normal part of the slow process of change. Sometimes it is simply a consequence of being reminded of something we once loved. But at other times it can be a result of mentally cherishing and nurturing the addiction while physically abstaining from it. Instead of asking God for a desire to hate sin at its roots, some people cling to the pleasant memories associated with their addiction. They remember that they once had a potent escape, whereas now they experience the pain of facing daily problems.

Don't forget, we sin because we like what it offers us—at least temporarily. When we stop sinning, temptation might linger as sin's residue in our hearts. The good news is that if it is true that temptations come from within us, that also means that deep change *at the level of temptation* is possible. "Each one is tempted when, by his own evil desire, he is dragged away and enticed. Then, after desire has conceived, it gives birth to sin; and sin, when it is full-grown, gives birth to death" (James 1:14–15). One of the great benefits of dealing with addiction at its roots is that we can fight against the behavior *and* the inner desire. And, as we have seen, this gives us the privilege of growing in our relationship with God.

What About AA?

AA has been helpful for many people. It provides accountability, mutual understanding in an environment that doesn't judge, and wonderful support for many people. It does not, however, strive to find distinctively biblical answers to the problems of life. As a result, it is bound to have some problems.

One of the problems is that its disease model doesn't really let anyone get to the heart of the matter. The addictive substance can be dangerous, but our hearts are more so. When we examine our hearts, we find that the greatest danger is that *we are hooked on ourselves.* If I am an alcoholic, my ultimate idol is not the bottle. It is *I.* I idolize *myself. My* desires are of first importance. *My* cravings rule—cravings for popularity, freedom from pain, revenge, or freedom from frustrations at home or work. Addiction is self-worship. This means that even if I give up alcohol, unless I deal head on with my biggest problem, I will never truly find freedom. I will just find something else to serve my desires.

A second weakness of AA is that its theory of change does not reveal the against-God nature of addictive behavior. Even though we are not always consciously aware that our addictions are disobedient before God, the reality is that they are. We are faced with a decision: Will I obey God or will I obey myself and my desires? Choosing one is choosing against the other. Forming an alliance with one is proclaiming war on the other.

A third weakness of AA is that Jesus is optional. If it is true that addictive behavior is rebellion against divine authority, then addicts have no hope but to run to Jesus for forgiveness, cleansing, and power. Addictions reveal a broken relationship with God; change comes by knowing the love of Jesus and being restored into that relationship.

A Proposal for Change

Here is a proposal. It is time for a change. *Disease* was once a metaphor, meaning that the experience of addictions felt *like* a disease. However, the metaphor has run amok and has led us to minimize some important features of addictions.

I suggest instead that we acknowledge that addictions are a *disorder of worship*. By doing this we are not ignoring the out-of-control experience of addictions, and we are not being blinded by the complexities of an addict's inner world. However, we are gaining important insights into our hearts and our relationship with God. Such a view of change immediately reminds us that we are in a battle between the worship of God and the worship of ourselves and our desires. It explains why we feel so guilty after a night of self-indulgence. And, since we don't have to wait for a physical cure to provide lasting change, it offers great hope through confession of sin, faith in Jesus' forgiveness of sins, and obedience.

But didn't we already try this once and find that it didn't work? Didn't AA come about because this more spiritual approach just made people feel guilty and less inclined to acknowledge their problem?

A Bible-based approach may have been less than helpful in the past, but not because of deficiencies in the Bible. Perhaps Christians used the Bible as a club rather than as words of life. Perhaps Christians approached addicts with a holier-than-thou attitude, not realizing that, at the level of the human heart, we *all* have the same problem and need the same help. Or perhaps Christians, not understanding the bondage of addiction, thought that a simple "stop it" would somehow end all addictive behavior.

With these sins of the church in mind, this biblical view can be offered with humility and grace, from one addict to another. Will people have trouble acknowledging their addictions? Probably. No one ever relishes having sins exposed. But when every Christian realizes that change in his or her own life is a process that takes more than saying "stop it," it will certainly create an environment where the norm is to bring problems out into the open.

Rethinking the Change Process

Once the problem is acknowledged, and once it is recognized as a problem of worship, there will be some new facets to our model of the change process. Foremost among these will be that the knowledge of God becomes our most important goal. After all, if the root of our problem with addiction is a problem of worship, then we need to learn who should be the true object of that worship.

As this idea takes hold of your heart, you will find that you feel more at home in a good church than in an AA fellowship. You will draw strength and wisdom from sermons, find encouragement in corporate singing, be spiritually fed in communion, and search the Bible for the living God. You will come to know more about the God who is bigger than you ever thought: bigger in justice, in power, and in love. You will see how his greatness works in your behalf. One problem with AA is that the "God as you understand him to be" is never large enough.

You will also find that you will have a deeper interest in speaking the truth. God is the God of truth. His language is the language of truth. It is impossible for him to lie. Chances are that this insight will reveal that you have not always been speaking God's language as you've talked about your life with alcohol or another addictive substance.

Aren't most addictions accompanied by lies, all the way from white lies to whoppers? Haven't all addicts at some time misled, changed the subject, justified, and blamed? At first glance, these lies don't seem like a big deal, especially compared with the substance use itself. They are simply cover-ups, ways that addicts protect themselves from the judgments of others. The biblical view, however, takes us further than that. The Bible indicates that lies hurt us, they are sins against others, and they are sins against God.

They hurt us in that lies deceive *us*, not just other people. They persuade us that we are on top of our problem. We think we can fool others, but we can't be fooled. With other people, the power of lies is obvious. Anyone who has been lied to knows that lies divide people; lies are the language of war. With God, lies provide evidence that our allegiances are not with him. Instead, they show that our allegiance is to Satan—the Father of Lies—and to ourselves.

The way out is to speak God's language, the language of truth. This is the way we can worship him. We can worship him by imitating him. After all, doesn't God always say to his people, "Be holy as I am holy"? Worship, after all, is not just singing with upraised hands. Worship consists of walking humbly before God in small steps of obedience. And truth-telling is part of that walk.

Speaking the truth goes even deeper than having true words come out of our mouths. It also means that we *believe* what is true. For example, it means that we believe the truth about ourselves. It means saying, "Lord, I confess that I have been committed to my own idols and desires."

Faith and Forgiveness

Along with truth about ourselves, we must know the truth about God. Specifically, we must know that God hates sin but freely offers grace and forgiveness to sinners who turn from it. Both these truths are essential. If God doesn't hate sin, then why should we? We would have very little reason to change. On the other hand, if we don't fully believe that God forgives us because of the death and resurrection of Jesus, then there is no point in trying to change. Without forgiveness, we would be condemned for our past and future sins, so that there would be no real hope. Satan would be unbridled, free to provoke despair and paralyzing guilt. With forgiveness, there is peace with God and a boldness to pursue the risky task of sobriety.

In short, Jesus, in his death for sins and resurrection from the dead, is the centerpiece of all change. We, as struggling sinners, must keep looking at him until we *see* and *know* that he is the fullest expression of God's hatred against sin and love for his people. We keep looking until we believe that Jesus paid the penalty for our sin and delights to give us power to fight against it.

If you waver, losing confidence that God's forgiveness covers your sins, there may be two reasons. First, you may think that God is no better than you. In other words, *you* couldn't imagine forgiving someone seventy times seven, so you can't believe that God would. If this is the way you are thinking, then you are believing a lie. God is not like us. His forgiveness is not like ours. Don't use your own weakness as the standard by which you understand God's greatness! Just listen as he reveals himself in his Word.

A second reason you may be hesitant to believe that God forgives you is that in reality, you are not taking your own sin seriously. You know what God says but you don't obey. In this case, the Bible says that you *should* have doubts—not about God's great forgiveness but about whether or not you are really God's child. Perhaps you are still living the lie. If so, you need to learn about God's love. It is a love that pursues rather than waits for you to be perfect. It is a love that sacrifices, even to the extent of Jesus' death on a cross. When you know this about the living God, you will begin to realize that "his commands are not burdensome" (1 John 5:3), and you will know that he gives power to fight sin. Then you can respond to God's love in obedience.

There is much more to say. This is just the bare outline of what I think the Bible says about addictions. Of the many other details that would probably interest you, I will just mention one. You should know that the Bible's method of change doesn't make life any easier. Instead, it equips us for battle. I knew a man who was, for a time, very discouraged that abstinence was so hard for him, even though he was dealing with the spiritual roots of his drinking. He had to learn that God's strategy for change is certainly no easier than any other strategy. In fact, it is probably more difficult. It means doing things that are very unnatural, such as loving another, forsaking our pride, speaking the truth, and doing battle with our desires. Abstinence is war. If it doesn't feel like war, you should be suspicious that something is not right. Yet this war is unique. Your most prominent weapon is your growing confidence in and love for Jesus. And you will notice a peace in your heart, even in battle, that comes from knowing that God's forgiveness is never a begrudging act. It is always done with pleasure and delight. His kindness is an everlasting kindness. And it is powerful enough to make changes at the deepest levels of our hearts.

Please consider these things. Let me know what you think.

Thank you.

Your brother in Christ,
Ed Welch

CHAPTER 11

FINAL THOUGHTS

DO you remember the questions from chapter 1?

"I think I have a chemical imbalance. What should I do?"

"Should my child be taking Ritalin?"

"Why is my father acting like this? Alzheimer's disease has changed him so much."

"Since his accident, my son has been fired from twenty-five jobs. Is he going to be living with us for the rest of our lives?

"I'm angry that God made me an alcoholic. Other people don't have to deal with this. Why did he give *me* this disease?"

"It's hard to stop cruising gay bars and getting pornography from the Internet. How *can* I stop when I have a homosexual orientation?"

The answers to these questions still are not easy, but they are available. They are available as we dig deeper into Scripture, trying to develop new applications of old truths. The old truths have been available for years: we are created as a unity of spirit and body. The applications have simply been waiting for these questions, and others like them.

If I had to choose two essential points from the previous chapters I would choose these two: First, be confident in what the Bible says. There is no reliable brain research that takes issue with timeless biblical truths. So don't be intimidated. Second, study people. Know their suffering. Don't assume that their abilities mimic your own. Study your children, your spouse, the students in your Sunday school class, and anyone else you have the privilege of encouraging with God's Word. As you know them better, focus more on their gifts—their brain strengths—than on their weaknesses.

As you do this, be strengthened by the fact that nothing—neither demons nor disease—can separate us from the love of Jesus.

> *Therefore we do not lose heart. Though outwardly we are wasting away, yet inwardly we are being renewed day by day. For our light and momentary troubles are achieving for us an eternal glory that far outweighs them all. So we fix our eyes not on what is seen, but on what is unseen. For what is seen is temporary, but what is unseen is eternal. (2 Cor. 4:16–18)*

Let this be your confidence and hope as you respond to the challenges of your own life and minister to others.

Edward T. Welch serves both the Christian Counseling and Educational Foundation (CCEF) and Westminster Theological Seminary. At CCEF he is, in addition to being a counselor and faculty member, the director of counseling and academic dean. At Westminster he is professor of practical theology. He joined both organizations in 1981.

In addition to writing *Addictions* and *When People Are Big and God Is Small*, Welch has contributed to several books, including *What's the Brain Got to Do with It?*, *Our Smallest Members*, *Leadership Handbook of Practical Theology* (vol. 2), and *Power Religion*.

Welch has written more than ten articles for the *Journal of Biblical Counseling*. Other periodicals to carry his essays include *Journal of Psychology and Christianity*, *Journal of Pastoral Practice*, *Journal of Biblical Ethics in Medicine*, *Carer and Counselor*, *Modern Reformation*, *New Horizons*, *American Family Association Journal*, *Spiritual Counterfeits Project Journal*, *Reforma Siglo*, and *Westminster Bulletin*.

At meetings of such organizations as the Christian Association for Psychological Studies, American Association of Christian Counselors, and Pennsylvania Psychological Association, Welch has presented papers.

After earning his M.Div. degree at Biblical Theological Seminary, Welch received, in 1981, a Ph.D. in counseling psychology (neuropsychology) from the University of Utah.

RESOURCES FOR CHANGING LIVES

Addictions—A Banquet in the Grave: Finding Hope in the Power of the Gospel. Edward T. Welch shows how addictions result from a worship disorder—idolatry—and how they are overcome by the power of the gospel. *0-87552-606-3*

Age of Opportunity: A Biblical Guide to Parenting Teens, 2d ed. Paul David Tripp uncovers the heart issues affecting parents' relationship with their teenagers. *0-87552-605-5*

Blame It on the Brain? Distinguishing Chemical Imbalances, Brain Disorders, and Disobedience. Edward T. Welch compares the roles of the brain and the "heart" in problems such as alcoholism, depression, ADD, and homosexuality. *0-87552-602-0*

Instruments in the Redeemer's Hands: People in Need of Change Helping People in Need of Change. Paul David Tripp demonstrates how God uses his people, who need change themselves, as tools of change in the lives of others. *0–87552–607–1*

Step by Step: Divine Guidance for Ordinary Christians. James C. Petty sifts through approaches to knowing God's will and illustrates how to make biblically wise decisions. *0-87552-603-9*

War of Words: Getting to the Heart of Your Communication Struggles. Paul David Tripp takes us beyond superficial solutions in the struggle to control our tongues. *0-87552-604-7*

When People Are Big and God Is Small: Overcoming Peer Pressure, Codependency, and the Fear of Man. Edward T. Welch exposes the spiritual dimensions of pride, defensiveness, people-pleasing, needing approval, "self-esteem," etc. *0-87552-600-4*

Booklet Series: *A.D.D.; Anger; Angry at God?; Depression; Domestic Abuse; Forgiveness; God's Love; Guidance; Homosexuality; "Just One More"; Marriage; Motives; Pornography; Pre-Engagement; Priorities; Sexual Sin; Suffering; Suicide; Teens and Sex; Thankfulness; Why Me?*

FOR FURTHER INFORMATION

Speaking engagements with authors in this series may be arranged by calling The Christian Counseling and Educational Foundation at (215) 884-7676.

Videotapes and audio cassettes by authors in this series may be ordered through Resources for Changing Lives at (800) 318-2186.

For a complete catalog of titles from P&R Publishing, call (800) 631-0094.